The Ten Commandments
Timeless Truths for Right Living

Terry W. Pollard

THE TEN COMMANDMENTS: TIMELESS TRUTHS FOR RIGHT LIVING
Copyright © 2020 by Terry W. Pollard
Published by Steuben Press
Longmont, CO 80501

ISBN-13: 978-0-578-71326-7

Cover design by Allen Porter / Springfield, MO

Printed in the United States of America

To my lifelong friend, teacher, mentor, supporter, and most importantly my loving and fabulous Mom, and the charter member of my "fan club" -
Eva Lavonne Pollard-Maddox
Thanks for leading the way as an example of godly, Christian living.

Acknowledgements

In writing a book there are many people who influence the author and make the book a reality. First of all, I would like to thank my now deceased pastor/preacher father, Raymond, who left me a lasting legacy of love and writing and inspiration for the writing of this book. His old message notes and thoughts around the Ten Commandments sprinkled throughout my collection of his inspired me to compile my own series of messages from which the foundation thoughts of this book are formed. I am forever grateful to my "preacher father."

Thank you to all my parishioners in the churches I have pastored during my ministry, who have been "captive" yet willing listeners and have given me input, encouragement, and continued motivation, as I shared series of messages on the Ten Commandments in a variety of ways – whether through Bible study, preaching, or writing.

Thank you also to my loving mom, Lavonne, as she is known to everyone, for always motivating me to keep putting my thoughts on paper and has been my constant encouragement in writing, wherever I have served and in whatever form my writing has been expressed.

Thanks also to my many friends and colleagues who have invested in my life, who read what I write, and have encouraged me to keep on writing and sharing my thoughts on paper.

Thanks to my dear wife and best friend for life, Diana, who single-handedly proves the existence of loyalty, learning, and wisdom. I love you.

Last, but by no means least, I have grace-filled gratitude for my Lord and Savior Jesus Christ who daily helps me focus on my relationship to Him as I seek to love God and love my neighbor.

FOREWORD

You are about to embark on a journey that could change your life. If your spirit is teachable you will come away from this reading with a changed heart.

Terry Pollard has drawn deeply from the well of the Scriptures. His rich spiritual heritage as a person and a pastor enables him to have a meaningful grasp of the Old and New Testaments and the relationship between law and grace.

In a day of political correctness and self-gratification being prominent, many people question the necessity and/or the relevancy of the Ten Commandments. The cultural chaos and moral cesspools in which people are swirling today evidence the need for a clear moral compass. The Ten Commandments are that divine truth.

Every person who claims to be a follower of Jesus Christ is called to be the light and salt for God in our culture. This is Christlike living. Not because we "have to" out of oughtness (Old Testament law) rather, because we "want to" (New Testament grace). This comes from a forgiven heart and the empowerment of the Holy Spirit.

I met Pastor Terry several years ago. It has been my privilege to partner in ministry with him on several occasions. I have eaten at his kitchen table, preached from his pulpits, spent some time with his family and have shared more lunches than he and I can recall or count. He is genuine. He loves God, the Church, and the Word. And he loves people and desires the best of God for their lives.

His quest regarding God's best for you is boldly proclaimed in *The Ten Commandments: Timeless Truths for Right Living*. This is not a common book. It will stretch your mind, challenge your spirit and compel you as a Christ follower so whether you eat or drink or whatever you do, to do it all to the glory of God (1 Corinthians 10:31).

You are about to get freshly blessed. Enjoy the journey and keep on living for Jesus.

A Fellow Pilgrim,

Dave Childers

Church of the Nazarene, Pastor

PREFACE

Maybe the most important words ever written are the Ten Commandments. These words changed the world when they were first presented from the finger of God at Mt. Sinai to the Israelites and delivered by Moses and they are changing even now. They are the foundation stones of civilization and culture. Furthermore, they are the blueprint and design for the Christian life. Given their staggering importance, you would think that all societies, educational and religious institutions, and individuals, would be intent on studying them. Sadly, this is not the case.

In a culture that largely exists as a desert of deception and lies, it's time to return to the basics of righteous living that find their foundation in what we know as the Ten Commandments. We are living in a time of moral crisis and our culture is being reshaped by degenerated thinking and decision-making. Many people today are looking for morality lite, everything you've ever wanted in a culture and less. No absolutes, no guidelines, and certainly no commandments.

Way too many people have strayed from absolutes. Moral relativism is the rule of the day. The foundations of truth have been washed away by the currents of secularism, pluralism, and privatization of truth. The waves are so strong that we seem unable to tell right from wrong any longer.

Because we have become a secular society committed to keeping peace at all costs, we have drifted into an age of "truth decay" and choices have become more difficult.

The vast majority of our culture sees the Ten Commandments as irrelevant. What does God know about my life, my situation, my trials, 3,500 years ago? You'd be surprised. Hence, this book is my attempt to demonstrate not only their relevance but also to show that the Ten Commandments are timeless, wise principles from the very mouth and finger of God. These principles can still show us how to live better and, in fact, live righteously as we continue to catapult in the twenty-first century.

This book had its genesis in several series of sermons and a series of writings for an adult Sunday school take-home paper as well as a series published in a denominational magazine some years ago. While I seek to provide some exegetical insight and theological depth, this book is not a book of exegesis or theology. Most fundamentally, it represents my heart – a practical approach for Christians who, out of love for the God who has saved us, sincerely want to walk in His ways and live out of love for Him and our neighbors.

The Ten Commandments spell out what love for God and our neighbor looks like. The content of our love for God and neighbor is not left for us to decide. Without divine holiness, love, and wisdom we will go wrong, and the Holy Spirit, who superintended the writing of the Scriptures, uses the Ten Commandments to guide us.

So it is that I hope by reading the pages that follow you will truly seek to live righteously in your own life, as I seek to do so in my life. How now shall we live? In complete obedience to God.

Warmly, Terry W. Pollard

CONTENTS

1 WHAT ABOUT THE LAW? 1

2 WHO'S ON FIRST? 14

3 IS THERE ANOTHER IDOL? 22

4 IS GOD'S NAME IMPORANT? 31

5 SUNDAY FUNDAY? 41

6 IS HONOR STILL HONORABLE? 57

7 BLOOD ON OUR HANDS 68

8 IS THE GRASS GREENER? 78

9 THE SIN OF STEALING 91

10 THE SANCTITY OF TRUTH 101

11 NEEDY OR GREEDY? 110

12 WHAT ABOUT JESUS? 122

The Ten Commandments

¹Then God spoke all these words:

² I am the LORD your God who brought you out of Egypt, out of the house of slavery.

³ You must have no other gods before me.

⁴ Do not make an idol for yourself—no form whatsoever—of anything in the sky above or on the earth below or in the waters under the earth. ⁵ Do not bow down to them or worship them, because I, the LORD your God, am a passionate God. I punish children for their parents' sins even to the third and fourth generations of those who hate me. ⁶ But I am loyal and gracious to the thousandth generation of those who love me and keep my commandments.

⁷ Do not use the LORD your God's name as if it were of no significance; the LORD won't forgive anyone who uses his name that way.

⁸ Remember the Sabbath day and treat it as holy. ⁹ Six days you may work and do all your tasks, ¹⁰ but the seventh day is a Sabbath to the LORD your God. Do not do any work on it—not you, your sons or daughters, your male or female servants, your animals, or the immigrant who is living with you. ¹¹ Because the LORD made the heavens and the earth, the sea, and everything that is in them in six days, but rested on the seventh day. That is why the LORD blessed the Sabbath day and made it holy.

¹² Honor your father and your mother so that your life will be long on the fertile land that the LORD your God is giving you.

¹³ Do not kill.

¹⁴ Do not commit adultery.

¹⁵ Do not steal.

¹⁶ Do not testify falsely against your neighbor.

¹⁷ Do not desire and try to take your neighbor's house. Do not desire and try to take your neighbor's wife, male or female servant, ox, donkey, or anything else that belongs to your neighbor.

- EXODUS 20:1-17 (CEB)

1

WHAT ABOUT THE LAW?

The Law became our custodian until Christ, so that we might be made righteous by faith (Galatians 3:24)

Very little is being heard or said these days about the Ten Commandments. In one church where I pastored, I preached a series of messages on the Ten Commandments. Before I began my series of messages, I polled the church people. The question I posed asked how many had ever heard a series of messages on the Ten Commandments. I was startled and disturbed to find that not one person in the entire congregation had ever heard a series of messages on the Ten Commandments. Furthermore, some of them proclaimed they had never once heard a message on any *one* of the Ten Commandments! You can guess I went ahead and preached my series of messages!

One would be hard pressed to find any other verses in the Bible that have had such a far-reaching impact as the Ten Commandments. They form the basis for so much of how we are meant to live and they are found in two primary locations in the Bible. In Exodus 20, God delivers them to His people; and in Deuteronomy 5, Moses rehearses them to the people before they enter the Promised Land. In numerous locations thereafter, the importance of individual commandments are repeated and emphasized throughout Scripture.

What do you know about the Ten Commandments? Are they still relevant or important in the 21st century? Consider this. During my years of ministry, I have heard many people make the declaration, "The Law isn't important to us anymore. That's just for the Old Testament. Now we are living in the day of grace. Keeping the Ten Commandments is just a legalistic requirement that is outdated and no longer meaningful." Such a statement among Christians often reflects a serious misunderstanding about what the Law of God is.

God never designed the Ten Commandments to be a rigid system of rules so our lives would be miserable. His commandments display His character. God knows that we live life to the fullest and live righteously and meaningfully and have the most joy if we live in a way that shows the character of God in all that we do and think. God knows how we think, how we respond in different situations, and what we need to have the healthiest relationship with Him and with each other. Therefore, He gives us warnings. These are healthy commandments. When people follow God's ways, their lives reflect that they are living their lives well and they are living righteously, according to His precepts.

Because the Ten Commandments reflect the character of God, they can be understood as the only valid standard of right and holy living. Break the Ten Commandments and judgment falls – and all people do fail to live by the Ten Commandments at some point in their lives. Only the God who gave them can keep them perfectly.

This is where the Gospel comes in. For when Christ died on the cross, He paid on our behalf the penalty we deserved for breaking those laws. This payment can be credited to our ledger if we accept – by faith – Christ's death for us.

God's love gave us the Law just as His love gave us the Gospel. There is no spiritual life for us save through the Gospel, which points us to Jesus Christ the Savior. That means there is no spiritual health for us save as we seek in Christ's strength to keep the Law and practice the love of God and neighbor for which it calls.

God's commandments give us a practical framework. They give us a grid by which to live our lives. They are a foundational blueprint and design for living. Although on our own we cannot keep them, if we understand their relevance and purpose, and as we ask for God's help, not only will our behavior change, but so will the way we make decisions.

God's rules prescribe the foundation upon which human society must be laid if justice, wholeness, and peace are ever to be achieved.

It is important to remember that the Law was given by God as a mirror to reflect our own lawlessness. It shows us how far we really fall from God's righteousness. Only through Jesus Christ can we ever gain a small grain of this righteousness.

Let's begin with this. Very simply, the Law can be typically divided into three parts: ceremonial, moral, and civil or judicial.

Ceremonial law was the type of law that related to Israel's worship, such as found in Leviticus 1-7, – laws pertaining to the kinds of offerings to be offered to God. It also related to temple regulations, symbols, sacrifices, worship, dietary laws and the nature of what was considered clean and unclean, and laws of purification. These were given to Israel in particular and considered temporary types, as types and shadows, prior to the Gospel and Christ's death on the cross. The laws pointed forward to Jesus Christ and were no longer necessary after Jesus's death and resurrection. Though we are no longer bound to them, the principles behind the ceremonial laws, to worship and love God, can still apply.

Moral laws, however, encompass God's declarations of what types of behavior are morally acceptable to Him. For example, behavior that He declares morally unacceptable includes rape (Deuteronomy 22:25-27), incest (Leviticus 20:11-12, 20-21), prostitution (Leviticus 19:29; 21:9), sodomy (Leviticus 18:22; 20:13), kidnapping (Exodus 21:16; Deuteronomy 24:7), perjury (Deuteronomy 19:15-21), witchcraft (Exodus 22:18; Leviticus 20:27), idolatry (Exodus 22:20; Leviticus 17:7). These are direct commands of God. The moral laws reveal the nature and will of God, and still apply to us today. We do not obey the moral law as a way to obtain salvation, but to live in ways pleasing to God.

Some Christians reject this view, claiming that it is based on the Old Testament law and that Christians are now under a new covenant – a New Testament, and so the Old no longer applies. It should be noted in answer to this that the moral law, expressing what God says is right and wrong, does not change from the Old Testament to the New. Whenever God says something is morally wrong, it remains wrong forever. Significantly, many passages in the New Testament affirm the moral law originally established in the Old Testament, such as 1 Corinthians 6:9-10; Galatians 5:19-21; Ephesians 5:3-5; 1 Timothy 1:9-10; Revelation 21:8; 22:15.

Civil or political-judicial law takes the rights and wrongs from the moral law and assigns penalties for their violations, such as the laws setting punishments for murder, theft, arson. This civil law dictated Israel's daily living, such as found in Deuteronomy 23-24, as an example – laws about escaped slaves, charging interest, neighbor's goods, pawning, loans, and payments for workers. But modern society and culture are in some ways so radically different that many of these guidelines cannot be followed specifically. The civil or judicial law applies to the arena of civil government and no other. And while the moral law remains unchanged across time, the judicial law can and does change.

For example, theft is always a violation of the moral law. But at the time of the Hebrews, the civil/judicial law punished it with economic penalties, which we know now is not the case. The moral violation is the same in all eras; the penalty is different. The principles behind the commands as they relate to civil law can well guide and do guide our conduct, however.

It should be noted that even the Ten Commandments – the epitome of the moral law – attach no judicial penalty to any of its commands. That is, while perjury is declared to be wrong, no specific punishment can be attached to it (or to any other moral misbehavior in the Ten Commandments). In short, the judicial law determines civil penalties for the moral law; and while the moral law does not change, the judicial law can. *(Noted in The Ten Commandments: The Moral Law for Nations – from The Founders Bible)*

The ceremonial and civil or political-judicial laws were purposeful, necessary but temporary, in contrast to the moral law.

The Ten Commandments refer to that part of the Law known as moral or ethical. The Old Testament moral law is where God reveals His nature, His will and lifestyle for humanity and guidelines for living.

Have you ever wondered why we should study the Ten Commandments – or this moral and ethical law designed by God?

It is right that we should acknowledge God's Law. The Ten Commandments have never been repealed. We need them. We are no better now than humanity was 3,500 years ago.

Where the Law's moral absolutes are not respected, people cease to respect either themselves or each other, humanity is deformed, and society slides into the degrading and defiling decadence of mutual exploitation and self-indulgence.

Jesus acknowledged the commandments, the Law. He taught the Law. "Don't even begin to think that I have come to do away with the Law and the Prophets. I haven't come to do away with them but to fulfill them. I say to you very seriously that as long as heaven and earth exist, neither the smallest letter nor even the smallest stroke of a pen will be erased from the Law until everything there becomes a reality. Therefore, whoever ignores one of the least of these commands and teaches others to do the same will be called the lowest in the kingdom of heaven. But whoever keeps these commands and teaches people to keep them will be called great in the kingdom of heaven" (Matthew 5:17-19).

We have instruction from the New Testament epistles. "Do we then cancel the law through this faith? Absolutely not! Instead, we confirm the law" (Romans 3:31). And we know also from Scripture that God has promised to punish those who disregard His law (Psalm 89:27-32).

Sounds important, doesn't it? Because it is important, it requires our consideration of these words written in stone by God forever.

In the Ten Commandments, God has told us how we are to relate to Him and to each other.

One of my favorite stories is about the pastor's son in his daddy's study. As a dedicated pro-lifer bends the ear of the pastor, he keeps saying, "You're right." Then a rabid pro-choicer comes in to plead the case and the pastor keeps saying, "You're right!" After they leave, the boy says to his daddy, "They can't both be right." And the daddy says, "You're right!"

That story betrays the moral relativism or ethical exceptionalism of modernity we face in our culture. Or as someone said during a board meeting early in my ministry, "I know that's what the Bible says, but I think . . ."

Everybody seems to be looking for exceptions to the rules – loopholes awarding the discoverer the license to do her or his own thing without regard to the expressed will of God as exemplified in Jesus and explained in the Bible.

We have entered into a time of moral crisis in our culture and the sad fact is we have entered into a time of moral crisis in the church as well. Stories and statistics about adultery, lying, and the individualized picking and choosing of doctrines abound. Many people today are looking for "morality lite" – no absolutes, no guidelines, and no commandments.

As a result of this thinking, at least three distinct philosophies have reshaped the morality of our culture today – secularism, pluralism, and privatization of truth.

Secularism is defined as "indifference to or rejection or exclusion of religion and religious considerations." With this understanding, laws are "right" because they seem rational and fulfill an immediate need, not because they follow God's commandments for right living.

For *pluralism*, Christian apologist Ravi Zacharias defines it as "the existence and availability of a number of world-views, each vying for the allegiance of individuals, with no single world-view dominant." In this view of pluralism, everyone's convictions, views and truth are equal. You have your view and I have mine. Both are equal in pluralism. No one way is seen as being the only truth. Moral relativism is the rule of the day. We no longer can tell right from wrong.

Privatization of truth simply means that you keep your truth to yourself and I will do the same. Since differences are private things, why should I invade your right to hold your opinion by trying to persuade you of my point of view. What's right for you is right for you. What's right for me is right for me.

This is the kind of thinking that has led to what I call "truth decay." Choices become more and more difficult because we seek to keep peace at all costs by maintaining an egalitarian approach to truth and keep it private. It is what F. LaGard Smith, in his book *When Choice Becomes God*, calls "a new revolution" based upon "the right for us to decide for ourselves, and the right of others to decide for themselves."

Sooner or later, everybody realizes living outside of God's will does not enable wholeness, happiness, joy, and security.

Is this what God intended? Is this God's plan for living? Is this God's plan for decision-making? Is this God's standard for right and godly living?

This is why we have the Ten Commandments. And this is also a reason why the commandments have a dual structure. It is generally noted that the first four commandments deal with human relationships to God (loving God), while the next six commandments talk about our interpersonal relationships (loving our neighbor).

The Decalogue (the word *decalogue* means "ten words"), as the Ten Commandments are correctly known, is unique because it demands exclusive worship of one God, bans idolatry, and institutes the complete Sabbath rest, among other things. And it compels us to love our neighbor in particular ways.

God states these commandments in absolute terms as the incontestable will of God rather than as time-conditioned case laws. As such, they address all God's people in every generation and emphasize the importance of communal and transgenerational obedience as well as individual responsibility.

The Law is given to administer God's grace to those who are already saved and to help them maintain the freedom that God already gave as a gift. Love and obedience are the proper response to God's salvation.

It is quite obvious that spirituality is all the rage these days. "I'm spiritual, but not religious!" is a common phrase, even if this kind of saying is impossible to achieve in practice. Even if you practice isolated spirituality, you are still following a religion of your own making. This kind of individualized religion is widely practiced in America, so it is a religion in its own right.

Instead of seeking out our own commands to follow, we should listen to what God has already set down for us. In the Ten Commandments, we learn from God what it means to live righteously, what it means to love God and love our neighbor.

Just when we are about to be driven to total despair by the law, Scripture assures us with the Gospel that God has sent His one and only Son to keep the Ten Commandments for us. Jesus came that we might have life – abundant life. Without the life of Christ, the Law brings us death. Even though we can't keep all of these rules, Jesus has kept the Law — all of it for us — by living a perfect, holy, righteous, obedient life. He never broke a commandment — not for a second — not even once.

So it is that we need to understand the root of true spirituality lies not in our keeping of these commandments, but rather in putting our trust, our faith, and our hope in the only One who has – Jesus Christ. God forgives you in Christ, and through His full forgiveness He enables you to begin to keep not only one commandment — but all the rest, too.

Jesus emphasizes the heart, or essence, of the Ten Commandments when He sums them up in Mark 12: "And you must love the Lord your God with all your heart, with all your being, with all your mind, and with all your strength. The second is this, You will love your neighbor as yourself. No other commandment is greater than these" (Mark 12:30–31).

This love for God and for others provides a moral compass to guide us, without which we are hopelessly lost.

That is why we must understand the importance of the Ten Commandments. The Ten Commandments are God's absolutes of how to live. They help us find the right direction in life. They provide direction for a directionless world. They provide a compass in a culture with no bearings. They help keep us headed in the right direction to reach God's best for us and live the life God intends for us to live. It is here that God lays out what our priorities should be, as well as what standards we are to follow.

The Ten Commandments spell out what love for God and our neighbor looks like. The content of our love for God and neighbor is not for us to decide. We are too sinful, too selfish, and too foolish to make our own decisions about these matters. Without divine holiness, love, and wisdom, we will go wrong, and the Holy Spirit, who superintended the writing of the Scriptures, uses the Ten Commandments to guide us.

10

I believe the Ten Commandments reflect our personal passion for God. How much do you love God? Do you love Him enough to put Him first in your life? Do you love Him enough not to get trapped by idolatry? Do you love Him enough not to misuse His name? Each of these questions is taken from God's Ten Commandments, and your answers are a gauge of your personal passion for God.

As you read the following chapters, perhaps the most important truth I can tell you is where we can find the fulfillment of God's Law. The Ten Commandments have their ultimate expression in the life of Jesus Christ. Paul stated in Galatians 4:4-5, "But when the fulfillment of the time came, God sent his Son, born through a woman, and born under the law. This was so he could redeem those under the law so that we could be adopted."

The Ten Commandments have a fuller meaning in Jesus Christ. To examine our Lord's life in the Gospels is to see a life in perfect obedience to the Law. He is the only One who obeyed perfectly. And it is Jesus Christ who came to redeem us, who are under the Law. And as He redeems us through salvation, we are adopted into His family!

As you read this book, allow your heart to be drawn to Jesus. God wants what you are about to learn to be written on your heart.

As we explore the Ten Commandments, we can explore them within a Christological context not as a list of *do's* and *don'ts* but as a prescription for positive and productive living, and more importantly, righteous living.

It has been said, "The holier we are, the happier we are." Living within God's will is an opportunity, not an obstacle, to experience existential and eternal well-being.

11

When our lives are in violation of the Law, we are not in God's will. Life, though, is not made up of just keeping the Law for keeping's sake.

We are not to focus on the Law, but rather we are to focus on the Savior, Jesus Christ. It is only through a relationship with Jesus Christ that we can understand and live by God's Ten Commandments. The Law will lead us afresh to Christ as we see our faces in the mirror of God's Word and we will realize the Law's vital function as it rules on our behavior.

I believe praying and working to incorporate this code of ethics into our lives will enable personal peace, found in and through Jesus Christ, while contributing to societal renewal.

That is when we will live righteously and according to truth.

What Early Church Fathers Said

CAESARIUS OF ARLES: *The two tablets of the law correspond to the two great commandments of the gospel. We should know that the ten commandments of the law are also fulfilled by the two gospel precepts, love of God and love of neighbor. For the three commandments which were written on the first tablet pertain to the love of God, while on the second tablet seven commandments were inscribed, one of which is "Honor your father and your mother." Doubtless all of the latter are recognized as pertaining to love of neighbor.*

AUGUSTINE: *Catechumens should be instructed on the whole of the Decalogue.*

(Ancient Christian Commentary on Scripture, Vol. III)

REFLECTION QUESTIONS

1. What was Christ's mission concerning the Law of Moses (Matthew 5:17-18)? How did He succeed (John 17:4, Romans 10:4, Luke 24:25-27)?

2. In light of how secularism, pluralism, and privatization of truth were identified in this chapter, how do you see them being evidenced in our culture today?

3. Why is an understanding of the Ten Commandments important for us today?

4. Think about the discussion of the ceremonial, moral and civil or judicial laws given in this chapter. How do you see those being realized in our culture today? What principles are at work yet today around these laws?

2

WHO'S ON FIRST?

"Do not have other gods besides Me" (20:3)

When I hear the first commandment, I am reminded of the old Abbott and Costello skit, "Who's on First?" The debate in this lively comedy centered around the name of the person on first base. Utter confusion reigned because it was never clear to one of these comedians who it was that belonged on first!

Other things pale in our lives until we settle the matter of who is on first. We need to know who is in first place in our lives. If anyone, or anything, occupies first place in our lives ahead of God, then our lives are out of control and out of balance. This is the gist of the first commandment. God tells us who must be first in our lives.

Synopsis. The first commandment demands exclusive worship of Israel's God, for this is the God who alone "brought you out of Egypt/slavery" (20:2). The expression "before me" conveys the idea that worshiping other gods is like committing adultery in front of one's spouse. This command assumes the existence of foreign gods whose worship threatens Israel's exclusive devotion to their one true God. John Wesley comments that this commandment calls readers to "set our affections entirely upon him" (*Notes,* Exodus 20:3), which would ensure obedience to the rest of God's commandments.

The command begins with the words, "I am the LORD your God." The first commandment asserts the aim of God to be sovereign, not only because of who He is (His character) but because of what He has done (His activity). Without these two, there is no basis or foundation for other laws. This demands that we ask, "What or who is going to be most important in my life?"

God said, "You must have no other gods before me." Most people, understandably, think this command only prohibits the worship of idols and the worship of gods such as the ancient pagan gods of rain, of fertility, or all the other nature and chief gods such as the Roman Jupiter and the Greek Zeus.

In Moses's day this command would have brought to mind the many specifically named gods worshiped among the nations. Amon-Re (the sun god), Osiris, Isis, Ptah, and Thoth were some of the Egyptian deities. The Baal gods and Asherah and Molech were worshiped among the Canaanites.

Today, in the Western world people no longer worship such gods. Because of this, many people think this first commandment is irrelevant to modern life. The irony is, however, this commandment is in many ways the mother of all the other commandments. God's first commandment establishes His sovereignty over our lives.

Why is this first commandment so relevant? Because today we have as many false gods as the ancients did, even if not called by the same names. We make a grave mistake in assuming that because our houses are free of idols fashioned of metal, wood or stone we have dealt with this and are ready to move on to the second commandment. The sobering truth is this: The "other gods" we worship are the things and persons (including myself) we place before God and claims our loyalty.

When anything else is worshiped, bad things result in our lives. Not only things that can lead to evil such as the worship of power, or race, or money, or flag, but also things that are seen as quite beautiful – such as art, or education, or love.

There are three meanings for the words "before me," as stated in this commandment. It can mean "*instead of me*." We substitute something else for God. It can mean "*in front of me*." We snub God. Or it can mean "*in addition to me*." We smother God out.

Why does God tell us He wants to be first? The simple answer is because He is the only true God. He deserves our worship. When we try to worship Him and still give other things priority, we worship two masters. Clearly, concisely, and conclusively, God's first commandment spells out one-way theology – "no other gods before me."

The Law is a mirror of our sin, and therefore, if we are told to "have no other gods" before God, we must already have them. What gods do people serve?

Some people serve the *god of pleasure*. Pleasure is like a drug. It often requires more to get the same effect. The law of diminishing returns says more and more is needed to get the same effect or high. This can include sensuality, sports, entertainment, drugs, or alcohol.

Some people serve the *god of possessions*. The gift of grab dominates many lives. These are people who place money and things first. They are always needing to have the right clothes and cars and shoes and houses. They are possessed by things. Proverbs tells us, "People's eyes are never satisfied" (Proverbs 27:20).

Some people serve the *god of "me first*." There are plenty of people who feel that the world revolves around them and that they must always come out on top. They have an aloof and elite air about themselves. Their conversation always revolves around their lives and interests. Conceit is the only disease that a person has that makes everyone around him or her sick.

Some people serve the *god of "my activities."* This involves anything that occupies the mind and life ahead of God. It simply means that we are so busy with other things that a relationship with God is pushed behind – there is just too much to do.

Susannah Wesley was the mother of John Wesley, the founder of Methodism, and Charles Wesley, who wrote over 6,000 hymns, many of which we still sing today. She got it right when she said, "Whatever weakens your reason, impairs the tenderness of your conscience, obscures your sense of God, takes off your relish for spiritual things, whatever increases the authority of the body over the mind, that thing is sin to you, however innocent it may seem in itself." That expression is encompassing of the gods that people serve – they become a sin to the person who serves these false gods.

We break this first commandment whenever we give anyone or anything more devotion or more authority in our lives than the Lord Jesus Christ. It has been rightly said that "Jesus is Lord of all, or He is not Lord at all."

Every major failure in our life traces to a failure at this point. It can be through false doctrines (someone has placed their own idea first), through sinful behavior (wrong priorities and actions), or through lack of spirituality (someone has put God and His work on the "back burner"). Whenever we put what we want above what we know is right, we have broken the first rule of right living. God is no longer first.

Our priorities really indicate who we are at the core of our being. What we make time for and what we invest our lives in shows where our true heart is. Whatever is your

17

highest priority will probably receive the vast majority of your discretionary time.

So, this means that even though I am in ministry I have to be careful that I don't let serving the Lord replace my fellowship with Him. I also have to be careful not to let the many possible demands on my time and service keep me from spending sufficient and proper time with my wife and family. These are sometimes difficult lessons to learn and choices to make. It means I have to make it a priority and do whatever I can to make it happen as my priority. It's not always easy to work these priorities into our schedule, especially with family or spouses, but it is very rewarding. It is, and must always be, a "first things first" priority.

Dwight L. Moody once said, "Trust in yourself, and you are doomed to disappointment; trust in your friends, and they will die and leave you; trust in money, and you may have it taken away from you; trust in reputation, and some slanderous tongue may blast it; but trust in God and you are never to be confounded."

I really like how Eric Ritz explained it in a sermon: "The Ten Commandments . . . were not given by an angry God, who wanted to deny freedom and joy to his people. They were given by a loving God to instruct his people to say, "No," to one way of life in order to say, "Yes," to a greater way of life."

The phrase "no other gods before me" literally says, "No other gods before my face." This familiar Hebrew idiom means, "in addition to me." We cannot allow anything or anyone to compete with our affection for God. We must forsake all other loyalties and put God first. It is a law of God that we cannot have split loyalties. Matthew 6:24 says, "No one can serve two masters. Either you will hate the one and love the other, or you will be loyal to the one and have contempt for the other. You cannot serve God and wealth."

Truly, we have to put first things first in our lives in order to fulfill this overwhelming standard God sets for our lives. When He is first, when we are Spirit-controlled, then we are in a right position and we are a good example of His life flowing through us, no matter how the world may think we should act. We can't afford to stumble because of divided loyalties. It can't be God on Sunday and the world the rest of the week. An old Irish proverb says, "A man who pursues two rabbits at once, catches neither."

There is no limit to the benefits that we enjoy as we seek to remain faithful in our loyalty to the Lord. God demands our exclusive loyalty, and we find that in this complete devotion to the one God there is freedom.

We can't fearfully tiptoe around the edge of our relationship with God simply because we do not know and have failed to comprehend just how trustworthy God is. There is no need to tiptoe around God. Just give Him first place in your life.

What Early Church Fathers Said

AUGUSTINE: *Let [my opponents] insist, if they like, in contradiction to their own assertion, that worship of the one true God and the prohibition against idolatry is not to be preached to the unbaptized by to the already baptized. Do not, however, let them any longer say to those who are going to receive baptism that they need be instructed only on belief in God and after the reception of the sacrament they will be taught the matter of living required by the second precept on the love of neighbor. For both are contained in the law which the people received after the Red Sea, that is, after baptism.*

GREGORY OF NYSSA: *Who then is our own God? Clearly, the true God. And who is the strange God? Surely, he who is alien from the nature of the true God. If therefore our own God is the true God, and if, as the heretics say, the only-begotten God is not of the nature of the true God, he is a stranger God and not our God.*

(Ancient Christian Commentary on Scripture, Vol. III)

20

REFLECTION QUESTIONS

1. In the discussion about the various gods that people serve today, which ones do you tend to struggle with in your own life? What can you do in your life to direct your attention away from false gods to the one true God?

2. What are intentional ways in your daily life that you can demonstrate to others that God is first place in your life?

3. In your own life, how has God worked powerfully for your benefit? How does thinking about God's faithfulness impact the quality of your worship?

4. What are some ways in which we make "self" an "other" god (Luke 9:57-62)? In your opinion, what are some common "gods" that people worship today? Why do you think people choose these other objects of worship?

5. Read Psalm 81:1–16. What does this psalm teach you about worship? How does it challenge you to worship better?

21

3

IS THERE ANOTHER IDOL?

"Do not make an idol for yourself" (20:4-6)

Maybe you have been to one of those old Ben Franklin 5 & 10 cent stores. You could walk into those stores and find a lot of "cheap" things. Now I guess we call similar stores The Dollar Tree – where literally everything you think you need costs only one dollar. Every summer I take several of my granddaughters on their annual visit to The Dollar Tree when they come to visit my wife and me. They really do pick out some nice things to bring home – but too many times they are broken before they ever leave to return to their parents after their visit. I have come to realize that the stuff that we buy at those stores typically don't last as long as we like.

Too many of us get sucked into dime store faith. We place our confidence in people and things that are cheap and wear out and don't last long

It has been said and is true that we become what we worship. Paul Scherer warns us: "The drift in human history is never away from religion itself, but only a religion with God at the heart of it toward a religion without any God at all except of our own making. The central problem is not Godlessness. It never is. The central problem is always idolatry." Millions are caught in this trap, worshiping and obeying something other than God.

That's why God gave us the second of the commandments. We probably think that the second commandment – "Do not make an idol for yourself" – doesn't touch us. After all, it's likely that none of us has in our homes an image of Jehovah God that is formed out of wood or stone, and none of us bows down before that kind of an object.

We don't really live in a culture or society that is inundated with "idols" like the golden calf the Israelites crafted at Sinai. Our idols don't come in the form of golden or bronze statues that are placed in the middle of a religious ceremony and all the people fall on their knees and worship it.

Synopsis. The second commands that we worship the right God in the right way (20:4-6). It is not enough to worship the correct God. We must worship the correct God *correctly!* Worshiping other gods or God through material images are banned not only because Israel's transcendent God has no material form (Deuteronomy 4:15-16) but because God made humans in God's image (Genesis 1:26); to reverse creation is to subvert its life-giving purpose. (cf. Romans 1:20-25).

It's a simple commandment. The second commandment of the Decalogue (Exodus 20:4-6) has not merely to do with images that are formed by human hands. The requirement here, stated positively, is that we worship God as He has commanded us in His Word. The second command was closely allied to the first: "You shall have no other gods before me" (Exodus 20:3). So important is the right worship to God that He has devoted one commandment of ten to this very concept. God commands rejection of anyone or anything that gets in the way of communion with Him.

Martin Luther once said, "Anything that one imagines of God apart from Christ is only useless thinking and vain idolatry." He also explained it this way in *The Large Catechism* (1529): "God will tolerate no presumption and no trust in any other object. He makes no greater demand on us than a hearty trust in Him for all blessings."

Anything we put before God is an idol whether we care to call it so or not. Some put family before God, some put their jobs before God, and a great many people put personal enjoyment before God. If these things become idols, they take the place of God. They, in effect, become God for us.

To obey this commandment sets us free from vain imaginations, strange superstitions, and improper and inadequate views of God so that we might learn to worship Him in spirit and in truth.

Just in case anyone assumes God is being a little picky about people who get brass plaques, dashboard deities, sports shoe superstars, and other kinds of hero worship, the commandment is a warning against placing trust in the untrustworthy.

So, what is *really* forbidden here in this commandment?

Image worship is forbidden. The erection and veneration of visible objects of worship comprises external idolatry and this is certainly and clearly forbidden. Back in the time when God gave this command, idolatry was blatant. This idolatry involved "gods" made from wood and stone and usually covered with some precious metal. Throughout the Bible, we read of many who made their living from idols. Terah, Abraham's father, worshiped other gods (Joshua 24:2), and Rachel stole the household gods owned by her father Laban (Genesis 31:19-37). More examples just like these can be found throughout the Old Testament.

The prophets condemned idol worship, and we know from the biblical record that idol worship was one of the reasons God let the Israelites be led into captivity by their enemies.

To kneel, pray, or burn incense before any man-made statue, whether saint or angel or image of Christ, is hard to reconcile with this command.

We must remember that God has revealed Himself to us, not in shapes of wood or stone, but in human form – in the unique person of Jesus Christ, who possessed both the divine and human natures. While we are to "fall from idolatry" we are to follow Christ who is "the image of the invisible God" (Colossians 1:15).

How does this relate to us? Most people in the Western world do not worship actual objects. But that doesn't mean we don't worship idols. We are spiritual beings, made for a relationship with God. So, this second commandment is not necessarily about shrines in our living room. It's more about understanding what or who is at the center of our hearts. What is it that fills that "hole in our soul" and meets our spiritual needs of legitimacy and meaning?

We can also understand that *irregular worship* is forbidden. Whenever we exalt liturgies, creeds, forms of ecclesiastical government, or church buildings, idolatry threatens us. If we go through the forms of worship perfunctorily, if we say prayers we don't feel, if we sing hymns we don't mean, if we render songs or preach messages simply because we are paid, if we give money because we're being watched or because it's deductible for income tax purposes, we are falling below genuine worship of the true God. The second command requires worship of God in spirit and in truth (John 4:24). Augustine said, "No words or pictures or monuments or whatever will ever come within reach of His dignity."

This commandment forbids *idle worship*. It condemns idleness, inactivity, and indolence in connection with our worship of God. It has to do with the energy we expend in our worship and devotion to the service of the true God.

Those who know God will honor Him with their bodies, their physical powers, and their strength. God has made the whole person - the body as well as the spirit for himself.

So many energies are devoted to the false gods of status: impressive homes, furniture, hobbies, cars, careers, and money. What a shot and shock the church would receive if people would transfer the same intensity and energy level to the extension of God's kingdom!

There are all kinds of God-substitutes. Knowledge, power, sex, friends, enemies, and on and on the list goes. Priorities are affected. Decisions revolve around our "god." Whatever is "god" to you will compel you to do what does the most good for yourself. You will focus on your needs and wants. You will focus on your own self-fulfillment. You will seek to satisfy your innermost desires.

Sadly, we as humans have a tendency to worship what is on the "outside," images, even though God has told us not to do this. This comes with our fallen nature. Our nature wants to do things its way and does not want to be told whom or what to worship. When we worship images of any kind, we lose sight of the thing that image represents. We begin to think that the image itself has power and personality.

The second commandment forbids the use of images as we worship God. However, the New Testament reveals that God has provided the only true and worthy image of Himself in the Lord Jesus, who is "the image of the invisible God" (Colossians 1:5). So then, our worship as we gather is to be framed by biblical principles. Christian worship is unlike any other event. Our objective in worship is not to make outsiders comfortable but to worship God in such a way that those outsiders may say, "Surely God is in this place."

God really means business on this commandment, as He does with all of them. But He gets especially pointed when He says in Exodus 20:5 that He is a jealous God. The word jealous can also be translated "zealous." It is not a negative term as we tend to view it today. It refers more to an action than to an emotion. It is not a statement of intolerance so much as it is a statement of exclusiveness. God sees His relationship with us to be like that of a marriage. No loving spouse would share their spouse with someone else. There are no substitutes for the attention, affection, and allegiance due to God alone.

Are there things that are competing for your allegiance? It could be one of a million different things in your personal life. Your job. Your car. Your hobbies. Your free time. Your money. Your responsibilities at work, home, or church. Anything that becomes so important to you that it interferes with your ability to obey the command to "love the Lord your God with all your heart, and with all your soul, and with all your strength" is an idol. The only way to deal with such a thing is to say, "I will not bow down to you."

And, if that thing is so tempting and so enticing that you know you cannot possibly live in its presence without giving in and "bowing down to it," then it's time to give it up. It is an idol. Get rid of it. As hard as it may be, whatever it is, give it up – and wipe away even the possibility of your actually "bowing down" to anything that is not God.

What is the shape of your god today? Whenever we allow God to be the hub of our life, the ride is so much smoother. It is not about the idols on your mantel. It is about understanding the truth that God has exclusive rights on our lives.

Be careful how you live and how you love. The Bible says in 1 John 5:21, "Dear children, keep yourselves from idols." That will mean daily decisions and daily choices. Obedience to this command requires it. But remember, every choice you make has a consequence.

It would be wonderful if what was said about the Thessalonians could also be said of us in our worship: "They tell how you turned to God from idols to serve the living and true God."

Worshiping God requires your complete surrender and devotion. The prize is eternal life beginning the moment you believe. No brainer, huh?

That's the way we live righteously.

What Early Church Fathers Said

ORIGEN: *[God] warns a man inclined to idolatry not to practice it. But when a man who is not so inclined but yet through cowardice, which he calls "accommodation," pretends to worship idols as the masses do, he does not, it is true, worship idols, but he does bow before them. And I would say that they who adjure Christianity in the courtroom or even before they are brought there do not worship idols, but they do bow down before them; for they apply to inanimate and unheeding matter the name of the Lord God, namely "God." EXHORTATION TO MARTYRDOM 6*

ORIGEN: *When men try to seduce us to apostasy, it is useful to reflect upon what God wishes to teach us when he says, "I am the Lord your God, jealous." In my view, just as the bridegroom who wishes to give herself entirely to him and beware of any relationship whatever with any man other than her husband, pretends, though to be wise, to be jealous – he uses this pretense as a kind of antidote for his bride – so the Lawgiver, especially when he reveals himself as "the firstborn of every creature," says to his bride, the soul, that he is a jealous God. EXHORTATION TO MARTYRDOM 9*

(Ancient Christian Commentary on Scripture, Vol. III)

REFLECTION QUESTIONS

1. Read Exodus 32:7-10. How does God describe the idolaters and their actions in this passage?

2. In your opinion, why is this second commandment needed? Since the first commandment is to have "no other gods," why does God give us a further prohibition against idols?

3. Since God forbids the worship of images, why did He give Moses the Ten Commandments written on stone tablets? What is the difference between a symbol and an image? How can we know when a treasured symbol has become an image?

4. For you personally, how is the second commandment significant? As you live out your faith, what impact does it make? Does this teaching highlight an attitude or habit you need to change?

4

IS GOD'S NAME IMPORTANT?

"Do not use the LORD your God's name as if it were of no significance" (20:7)

"The purpose of words," said a cynical diplomat, "is to conceal thoughts." As it relates to how we actually talk and communicate, that statement is too true to be good. Think about how often we talk for effect, saying to each other things we really do not mean and most likely cannot defend. And we often give assurances that we have no real intention to fulfill.

Have you ever wondered why our lives are too often littered with promises that, whether from malice, bad management, self-seeking or sheer carelessness, are not kept? The Bible takes promises very seriously. God demands faithfulness to our vows. This is because trustworthiness is part of His image which He desires to see in us.

The third commandment reminds us of the evils of misusing God's name. The name of God is routinely misused by all ages and in all places. When our language becomes careless, our living becomes careless. The language of the streets has slipped into our living rooms. And when we lose respect for God, we lose respect for each other.

It is important to consider how we are to use God's name. When we misuse His name, we hurt ourselves. If we use His name correctly, we find victory.

Synopsis. The third commandment prohibits wrongful use of the divine name (Exodus 20:7). It may include use of God's name in false oaths (Deuteronomy 5:20; Psalm 24:4; Jeremiah 5:2; Hosea 4:15; 10:4), false report (in witness or lawsuit), idol worship (Exodus 32:4; 1 Kings 12:28), pagan rituals, magic or witchcraft.

The third commandment states: "Do not use the LORD your God's name as if it were of no significance; the LORD won't forgive anyone who uses his name that way" (Exodus 20:7). In place of "no significance" as translated in the *Common English Bible*, the *Authorized Version* (King James) uses the words "in vain" – which means "for unreality." Vain means empty, idle, insincere, phony, frivolous, lacking in reality or truth. What is forbidden is any use or involvement of God's name that is empty, frivolous, or insincere. This command is talking about misusing the name of God. It is talking about using the name of God without attaching holy meaning and significance to it.

In biblical usage, a name was an expression of character standing for the person. Trace the names throughout the Bible and you will discover that names had significance. Not just the names assigned to God, but names given to people.

More than 300 names for God appear in the original languages of the Scriptures. All that God is and all that God does can be comprehended in His many names. He is "The Almighty God," the "Everlasting God," the "Lord Jehovah," the "Most High God," "Jehovah-shalom," "Jehovah-nissi," "Jehovah-jireh," the "Lord God of hosts"— and on and on the list goes. Every one of the names for God used in the Bible describes some attribute of His being and demands our reverence toward Him.

To trust in the name of God is to trust in God Himself. To take God's name in vain is to treat God lightly, irreverently, or insincerely. To take God's name in vain means that one places no significance to God.

This commandment reminds us then, that in all our words we should be aware of the reality of God. We should be aware of the awesome and holy significance of God. God's name means something and it should mean something to us as well!

Let's dig deeper. Why should we take God's name seriously, as this commandment requires?

We take it seriously because the name of God reflects His nature and character; because His power and presence are very real; because of God's reputation in our community; because to know God's name is a privilege – it means that He desires to have a relationship with us.

When we consider this commandment, we often think in terms of verbal profanity. But there is more in view here than just verbal profanity. The third commandment is much broader than that.

This commandment not only deals with our speech, but also with our lifestyle. It deals with our lips and our lives, with our words and our walk.

The point of this commandment can be stated quite simply. It is not just about saying God's name; it's about showing reverence for God's nature.

To take God's name lightly is (1) to scorn His character and nature; (2) to underestimate His power and show contempt for His presence; (3) to misrepresent His reputation to the human family; and (4) to treat the awesome privilege of His relationship lightly.

Such an offense is so serious that the command is accompanied by a warning: "The LORD won't forgive anyone who uses his name that way."

In no way is this an unpardonable sin, as if we can't be forgiven if we break this command. Rather, the intended emphatic use of the words "not forgive" in the *Common English Bible* or the word "guiltless" in the *Authorized Version* is meant to specifically emphasize that this is in no way a casual thing; this is an important thing and God will, in fact, absolutely hold you accountable for how you use His name.

God has revealed His nature to us through His name. We should readily see that God does not want His name taken lightly. We must understand clearly that God is holy, and His name in holy. To use His name flippantly and in disrespectful ways show that we do not take seriously the greatness and the awesome holiness of our God.

So, how is it that we can misuse God's name?

We can misuse God's name by *lying under oath*. If we say, "So help me God, this is true," either formally in a court of law or informally as a matter of conversation and then proceed to tell a deliberate falsehood, we have dishonored His name.

We can misuse God's name by *imploring God's name in trivial ways*. If we use God's name to reinforce our opinions, claiming to know how God reacts to matters on which we have strong feelings, we use His name lightly. To ask God to protect you when you are violating laws is to use God's name for an unworthy end or trivial way.

We can misuse God's name *carelessly in worship*. What if we "invoke" the name of God in worship as if the name alone is enough to guarantee God's blessing on our gathering and our lives – even if our attitudes throughout the week suggest that we don't believe the things that the names and titles of God suggest about Him? What if we sing "Have Thine Own Way, Lord" when we have no intention of letting Him have His way with us? What if we sing "I Surrender All" while clutching it all in our fist, refusing to give it up to Him? What if we sing "Trust and Obey" and then fail to do exactly that? We must not sing "Sweet Hour of Prayer"— and then be content with less than five minutes of prayer a day. We must not sing "Blest Be the Tie That Binds"— and then let the least little offense sever that bond. We must not sing "Cast Thy Burden on The Lord"— and then worry ourselves into nervous breakdowns. Let it be said that we have violated His name if this is how we choose to respond to the affirmations of God's name and character.

We misuse God's name *carelessly in conversation*. God's name is too often degraded to the status of an exclamation point in conversation, such as "Good God!" or "Oh, Lord!" To a question, the reply may be given, "Only God knows." Such an answer can be an honest reference. Too often, however, it is just a flippant retort with little meaning and used as a careless expression without any careful or holy thought.

We misuse God's name in *slang expressions*. Slang expressions are often substitutions or variations of powerful swear words. Whether it is golly, gee, gee whiz, jeeze, jeepers creepers, or any other such derivative, we diminish the value and importance of God's name by such flippant and thoughtless remarks sprinkled in our daily conversations.

Language experts say that over the years "God" became "by gad" and "by golly" and "by gum." "Jesus" became "gee whiz" and "jeeze" and "gee whillikins." "Christ" became "cripes" and "jiminy Christmas" and "jeepers creepers." "Lord" gave way to "lawdy" and "laws sakes." Kicking these expressions around in one's everyday conversation can hardly be pleasing to God.

We misuse God's name by *using profanity*. It is always wrong to swear and curse and use God's name in a blasphemous way.

Ours is a cursing age. A man has a flat tire and he curses the tire. She stumbles over a chair in the dark and she curses the chair. He has an audience of a few people that he wants to entertain, and so he thinks he must swear. Everyday profanity – for example, "Oh God," "Oh, Jesus Christ," and any derivatives – may not be the worst of sins, but there is no doubt that this use of God's name is a nasty breach of the third commandment, since it expresses neither faith nor worship.

Some say they don't mean anything by their swearing, or by using the substitutes — but Jesus condemns even idle words. Those words "which you don't mean" are the very words which Jesus condemns. If you don't mean them, then don't say them!

When we consider that Jesus came from heaven to shed His blood for us, it is quite bewildering that anyone should use that name or God's name as a curse word or with utmost profanity. The words "God" or "Jesus" should never be hurled as curses from the mouth. Swearing is neither smart, sensible, nor worthwhile. It certainly violates God's Word.

So, how then do we honor His name?

We honor it by *living a life that is committed to obedience* to the commands of Scripture. We honor it by studying those commands, by studying God's Word.

We are to *praise* His name. Worship. Give thanks. Lift up prayers of gratitude to Him for all He has done and all He will do. We keep the third commandment not only in the way we speak to God but also in the way in which we speak about Him.

36

We are to *celebrate* His name. This is worship, too; specifically, it is worship that flows from the heart and not from the folded order of worship in your hands. Learn the names of God in Scripture and discover the meaning of who God really is as revealed through His names.

We are to *invoke* His name. Stand firm on the promise of Christ who said that wherever two or three gather "in (His) name," He is there with us. Utilize that promise by turning to God prayerfully whenever the occasion arises.

We are to *share* His name. We reveal our commitment to the positive side of this commandment not only in our talking but also in our walking. Share it verbally and share it by living example, by showing others in practical terms how a life is saved by the Savior, how a person is transformed by the Good Shepherd, how a spirit is uplifted by a touch from the Prince of Peace, how fears are calmed by the presence of the Almighty, how lives can be changed for eternity by the sacrifice of the Lamb of God.

Use the name of God, carry the name of God, wear the name of God like it means something to you. Respect and awe for His divine name will grow, making it difficult if not impossible to use it frivolously.

I am reminded of the story told about the surrender of the Confederacy at Appomattox Courthouse as the Civil War concluded. General Grant was an unusual man. Knowing the war was over and the victory was his, he showed great – and unusual – kindness and respect toward the chief general of the Confederates. He allowed General Robert E. Lee to ride freely in and out of the area. He also allowed the Confederate men to keep their possessions and horses. Grant gave them food because they were hungry and let them all go home undisturbed.

Lee was permanently touched by Grant's kindness. After the war, Lee took a job at Washington University in Virginia. On one occasion one of his fellow instructors, also a Southerner, began to speak poorly of Grant to Lee (assuming he'd receive a sympathetic audience). Lee turned, looked the man straight in the eye, and said, "Sir, if you ever again presume to speak disrespectfully of General Grant in my presence, either you or I will sever his connection with this university." Because General Lee had received such kindness from Grant, he treasured and protected the good name of the one who had showed him kindness.

And when it comes to the name of the LORD our God, so should we!

Think often of God. Think of who He is — the omnipotent, omniscient Creator of the universe. Think of what He has done — His watch care and His providence over our lives day by day. Think of how Christ suffered — the shame and buffeting and pain — all for us.

As you think upon His being, there will grow in your heart, a respect, awe and reverence for His name.

What the Early Church Fathers Said

EUSEBIUS: *Here too the Lord himself teaches in the passage before us about another Lord. For he says, "I am the Lord they God," and adds, "You shall not take the name of the Lord your God in vain." The second Lord is here mystically instructing his servant about the Father, that is to say, the God of the universe. And you could find many other similar instances occurring in Holy Scripture, in which God speaks as if in a second voice about another. The Lord himself speaks as if about another.*

AUGUSTINE: *The third commandment: "You shall not take the name of the Lord your God in vain; for whoever takes the name of the Lord his God in vain will not be purified." The name of the Lord our God Jesus Christ is Truth: he himself said, "I am the truth." So truth purifies; futility defiles. And because whoever speaks the trust speaks from what is God's – for "whoever speaks falsehood speaks from what is his own" – to speak the truth is to speak reasonably, whereas to speak futility is to make a noise rather than to speak. Rightly, because the third commandment means love of the truth, the opposite of that is love of futility.*

(Ancient Christian Commentary on Scripture, Vol. III)

REFLECTION QUESTIONS

1. In the original language, the word for "misuse" (also translated as "take in vain") has a wide range of meanings. In your opinion, what are some common ways that people misuse or dishonor God's name?

2. This commandment carries a severe consequence: "The Lord will not hold anyone guiltless." Why do you think this is significant? Does this mean God won't forgive people who misuse His name?

3. This commandment assumes people will use God's name correctly. In your opinion, what does it look like for a person to honor God's name?

4. Take a quick inventory of your life: How well do you represent the name of God? Do people know you are a Christian? Are your good deeds done in His name?

5

SUNDAY FUNDAY?

"Remember the Sabbath day and treat it as holy" (20:8-11)

I well remember in the earlier decades of my life growing up, very little happened on Sunday except church, Sunday school, and the family meal. We didn't play basketball. We didn't work around the house or outside. We didn't go to the retail store to do shopping. We didn't buy gas at the local convenience store. We didn't eat out at the local restaurant. You really didn't have to be a philosopher in our household to figure out that Sunday was a different kind of day.

In no way am I begrudging or judging the reality that Sunday was so different from the rest of the week. It was so compelling. But, from my upbringing in those earlier days, I got a message about life that stayed with me up to my current reality. Life, I learned young, is about more than noise. Life is about listening to the music of the soul. Work is important but it can be a distraction from meaning. Reflection is the essence of being human.

The polling data tells us that Americans are a religious people, the large majority of whom claim to attend church with some regularity, they believe in God, and claim to pray daily. But think about it. You maybe wouldn't know it in your community from a typical Sunday, where the malls are clogged, the movie theatres are full, and the roads crawling with cars and bikers. Though we all might still possibly

41

remember the Sabbath day, in the land of perpetual fun we surely don't appear to keep it holy.

That reflection brings us to the fourth commandment. It is the longest of the ten, comprising at least four verses. A shortened version of the commandment simply states: "Remember the Sabbath day and treat it as holy."

Step back a bit in time and history of Scripture. On the Sabbath, life changed. The privileges and expectations of standard roles and relationships ceased. The world, as it operated from the end of one Sabbath to the beginning of another, halted, stopped in midair, suspended itself over time.

The Jewish concept of Sabbath, it seems, was unique. What's even more impacting is that it was not only a philosophy of life; it was a precept, a principle, a teaching. It was a wisdom word, a guide to the good life. It was a reminder to us that we are all "made in the image of God," human beings, equals.

But in this new world of ours, Sabbath means less and less every day. Is this day supposed to be a holiday or a holy day? Are we really expected, considering our busy schedules, to take off one day in seven? Are we really expected to enter the world of *being*, rather than just *doing*? Is this biblical injunction about the Sabbath applicable still today?

Because some have hedged the Lord's Day, as we often call it, with the burden of human rules and regulations, we must refuse to react by dispensing with "the Day" but instead by clearing the confusion so as to reveal the beauty and benefit to body and soul. Once we understand this beauty and benefit, I believe we will recognize how life-changing, even world-changing, the Sabbath commandment is. And we will begin to appreciate how relevant it is to our own lives.

Synopsis. The fourth commandment charges God's people to "treat" the Sabbath day "as holy" by ceasing all work (20:8-11), even during the busiest agricultural season, when one would be most tempted to work nonstop. Acceptable Sabbath to the Lord releases the seventh-day holiness and blessings into the other six days, making the work fruitful and satisfying. Worshipers joyfully imitate the Creator of the universe, who first took the Sabbath rest (Genesis 2:2 3). Having been made in God's image, humans are called to be like God (by being holy) and act like God (by resting and giving rest to fellow human beings, livestock and the land). The act of imitating God's being is God's gracious means of restoring human dignity and identity as God's children.

The word "sabbath" does not mean a particular day. It does not even mean "seventh" (as some people wrongly suppose). The words "sabbath" and "seventh" do not come from the same root word. They have no relationship to each other. This word "sabbath" simply means "rest" or "a cessation from labor"— and it does not have to be on the seventh day.

Sabbath, it is clear, comes out of Hebrew respect for the sacredness of all life and the grounds of human dignity. Sabbath is not a day of "rest" because people are tired. It is a day of rest because people are human and ought not to be driven to death, because every living thing requires time to renew itself, if not physically, certainly spiritually; if not spiritually, at least physically.

Joan Chittester, in her book *The Ten Commandments: The Laws of the Heart*, writes, "It is a day of protest against the enslavement of peoples anywhere. It is a day of reflection on the life that makes humanity more than simply an exercise in survival. Sabbath says that we must take the time to remember that we came from God and to determine what we are doing daily in the process of returning there."

Unfortunately, we stand on the brink of losing this concept. We have enslaved ourselves as well as failed to notice the new kinds of slavery that are being created around us. We have forgotten who we are – that we are humans, that we are "made in the image of God" – so we have, of course, forgotten who the other is as well.

The Fourth Commandment says, "Remember the Sabbath day." It does not say, "Remember the seventh day," nor does it say, "Remember the first day." We are to "remember the **rest** day, and to keep it holy." The Jews observed the seventh day (in memory of the finished work of creation); the early church commemorated the first day (in memory of the finished work of redemption).

What is being mandated is that the divine pattern be followed. As God rested after six days of work, so His creatures set apart one day in seven expressly for rest and worship. It is very obvious from the Scriptures that God expects His people to observe a sabbath (to observe one day in seven). The Mosaic (Jewish) Sabbath was set within the framework of ceremonial laws which the first Christians soon realized had been fulfilled in the Lord Jesus and were no longer mandatory. It is altogether proper that we keep the first day of the week because that is when Jesus by example met with His disciples.

Some say that observing the Sabbath in this present age of grace is not very important. They say that the Ten Commandments are all repeated in the New Testament, except the Fourth Commandment. But such statements are misleading. The Fourth Commandment is not repeated word for word in the New Testament, but it is exalted in the New Testament just as it was in the Old Testament. Jesus did with this commandment what He did with the other nine commandments. He expanded its scope and explained its typical meaning.

Let's begin by asking a simple question and then expound on it a bit here. Why is this Sabbath commandment important?

As a starting point, Sabbath says that we are made for reflection and that unless we do it, unless we begin to reflect on what we are doing as humans to other humans, to the earth, to the cosmos, we become nothing but cogs in an enslaving system. Sabbath reminds us that time is the only resource we really have and that we must teach ourselves to use it well. In fact, Jesus said that God had set aside the day for the benefit of man.

The Sabbath is taught in the Bible from Genesis to Revelation. It was established at creation (Genesis 2:2,3); reiterated as moral law at Mt. Sinai (Exodus 20:8-11); administered by Jesus, the Lord of the Sabbath (Matthew 12:8); identified as the first day of the week in commemoration of the resurrection (John 20:1, 19, 26); observed by the Church (Acts 20:7; 1 Corinthians 16:2); and is descriptive of our hope in heaven (Hebrews 4:9).

Jesus, Scripture is clear, kept the Jewish Sabbath. However, in the early church, as those first Christians found themselves further and further from the synagogue, especially those outside of Jerusalem, they became more Christ-centered and more committed to Jesus as the Messiah.

For Christians, and for clearly theological reasons, "Sabbath" became "Sunday" by the second, third and fourth centuries. The Jewish Sabbath almost disappears from recorded Christian practice after Christ's resurrection. The followers of Christ very quickly chose the first day of the week as their special day when they would meet to worship God. In doing so they were recognizing and establishing the significance of the Resurrection. The life of Jesus was its centerpiece. Resurrection trumped death and life was eternal. But the concept remained the same: life was not to be taken lightly, not to be taken for granted. Regular reflections on its meaning, its purpose gave it unending energy and renewed direction. Sunday Sabbath for the Christian meant celebration, yes, but it also meant remembrance. By using *Sunday, Sabbath* and the *Lord's Day* interchangeably, we are simply affirming the abiding place of one day in seven for rest and worship.

Consider several other observations. *First*, perhaps more than any other commandment, the Sabbath elevates the human being. How so? For nearly all of human history, life consisted overwhelmingly of work. In effect, humans were beasts of burden. This commandment and only this commandment changed all that by insisting that people cease working one day out of seven.

Second, more than any other commandment, the Sabbath Day reminds people that they are meant to be free. As the second version of the Commandment – the one summarized by Moses in the Book of Deuteronomy – states, "Remember that you were slaves in Egypt." In other words, remember that slaves cannot have a Sabbath.

As a side note here I might add, that in the biblical view, unless necessary for survival, people who choose to work seven days a week are essentially slaves – slaves to work or even to money, but slaves nonetheless. The millionaire who works seven days a week is simply a rich slave!

Third, it needs to be noted that the Sabbath almost singlehandedly creates and strengthens family ties and friendships. When a person takes off work one day every week, that day almost inevitably becomes a day spent with other people – namely family and/or friends. It has similar positive effects on marriages also. Ask anyone married to a workaholic how good it would be for that marriage if the workaholic would not work for one day each week – and you can appreciate the power of the Sabbath Day.

One other note about this Sabbath commandment. You don't have to be a Jew, a Christian or even a believer in God to derive these benefits of the Sabbath. But the reality is that those who believe the Ten Commandments were given by God are the ones who have kept the Sabbath alive.

So, the Sabbath Day is designed for relaxing the body, refreshing the mind, and for restoring the soul. Part of the Fourth Commandment says, "Six days you shall labor." Life is not a grand frolic; God expects every able-bodied person to work; but then, after six days of labor, a day of rest is necessary for good health.

Significant figures in history have certainly felt that keeping the Sabbath had great significance. Voltaire said, "I can never hope to destroy Christianity until I first destroy the Christian Sabbath." Gladstone said, "Tell me what the young men of England are doing on Sunday, and I will tell you what the future of England will be."

Is Sunday your "fun day?" Is that the day you keep for yourself? For your pleasure? For your chores?

The Sabbath testifies of God's goodness in His creation and of His saving mercy to His people. Sabbath keeping honors God as our Creator and Redeemer. It reminds us of how God has saved us in the death and resurrection of

Jesus and encourages our hope of heaven. It is a day sanctified by Christ himself who comes among His people when they gather for His worship. Sabbath observance lies at the heart of our obligations to worship. Biblical faith is seen when we forsake all else to promote that which is of supreme importance, the worship of God.

So, what are the implications for observing and remembering the Fourth Commandment about Sabbath keeping for our lives?

In a particular scope of this command, it means we *cease from work*. Physical rest is required by the fourth commandment, "Do not do any work on it" (Exodus 20:10). Just as our automobiles need periodic maintenance, so also do we. There is a tremendous "maintenance law" for cars, and there is a "maintenance law" for people, too. It is more than simply a tune-up, however. It is a plan for our total welfare.

The truth God is communicating to us is that there is more to life than labor. God modeled this truth through His own behavior in creation. Exodus 20:11 says, "Because the LORD made the heavens and the earth, . . . but rested on the seventh day. That is why the LORD blessed the Sabbath day and made it holy."

Why did God rest on the seventh day? Was it because He was tired? Was it because He couldn't think of anything else to do? We know that God did not need six days in which to create the world. And He did not need to rest on the seventh day – the Sabbath. God did these things in order to give us an example. He wanted to show us that there is a time for work, and a time for rest from work.

As we noted earlier, the word Sabbath in Hebrew comes from a root word that means "rest." Rest in a spiritual sense is also implicit in this command, because the resurrection brought the stamp of divine approval on Christ's finished work in which we rest (Hebrews 4:8-11).

The ordinary routines of life are to be suspended not as an occasion for laziness but in order that we might ponder God's works, participate with His people in worship, and pursue opportunities to do good to others.

Jesus's Sabbaths were days, not for idle amusement, but for worshiping God and doing good – what the *Shorter Catechism* calls "works of necessity and mercy." Physically, we need a change. Admittedly, some jobs of "mercy, compassion and safety" (works of piety and mercy and necessity) must be done on Sunday. But where possible the believer should abstain from the command and servile tasks of life, whether employed by others or at home. Jesus's disciples plucked corn on the Sabbath (Matthew 12:1-8). Whatever we do should not return us to work Monday more tired than we came home Friday. Like the other commandments, the fourth is designed to enable us to serve our Creator better.

Sunday is the day that sees us "safely through the week." Keeping this day rest-filled and holy is what one person called "a mental bath."

It is interesting to note that every culture in the world organizes their schedule around a seven-day week. Historians who reject the Bible have always been puzzled concerning the origin of this system. The seven-day week does not fit into the 365 ¼ days of the solar year nor the lunar month of 29 days. The seven-day week could only have come from the pattern set by God as a reminder of the seven-day creation period. Throughout documented history, experience has proven the seven-day week to be the most satisfactory way of organizing human life.

For example, both the French and Russian revolutionaries tried to abolish it, as did the government of Sri Lanka (Ceylon) in the 1960s. In each case it was a disaster. One rest day out of eight or ten days is too long an interval – one day in six is too short - one day in seven is just right. All three governments had to revert to a seven-day week. How interesting that even communist and atheistic cultures are forced to acknowledge the Creator in how they organize their calendars – all based on this commandment!

There is a flip side to this commandment. God not only wants us to be benefited by an absence of servile work, but also to be blessed by an accent on worship.

Is this day a holiday or a holy day? The word "holy" means that it is to be a day dedicated to sacred use. The word translated "holy" literally means "to set apart" or "different." The Sabbath is different in the sense that it especially belongs to God. It is a day that we keep separate and different from other days.

This special day then is a blessing for us in several ways. We are blessed physically, emotionally, and spiritually. God established the priority of a special day of our blessing and benefit. The writer of Hebrews commands us that we should not neglect the corporate gathering together as the community of faith. God knows we not only need rest, but we also need special communion from Him, which only comes from worship. In that sense, we have labeled it as "The Lord's Day."

We must not neglect it. Situations that cause us to miss the gathering of the church should be the exception, not the rule. Billy Graham once said, "Jesus spoke about the ox in the ditch on the Sabbath. But if your ox gets in the ditch on every Sabbath, you should either get rid of the ox or fill the ditch."

When we gather together in Jesus's name, we must remember that God is among us. There is a special presence reserved for the corporate gathering for His people. A certain anointing of the Holy Spirit is reserved for God's people when they gather.

Our bodies need rest. But more desperately than our bodies needing rest, our spirits need worship. That does not mean we do not worship during the week. But there is something especially refreshing and dynamic about corporate worship. It is a time in which we can, together with God's people, singularly devote ourselves to the noblest task of exalting the name of our God. In so doing, our lives are changed.

What affects one aspect of our being also affects the others. When you are spiritually and emotionally refreshed, your physical being responds. We need this special day.

So how can we keep the Sabbath (Sunday) a special holy day?

We can set this day apart as a *priority day*. Treat it as a special day. Block it out on your calendar and then don't let anything or anyone interfere with it. You have an appointment with God that day.

Steve Zeisler, one of the teaching pastors at Peninsula Bible Church in Palo Alta, California, said in a message on this commandment: "If the same command were given to us today, it would mean that one day every week we should not be thinking about getting prepared for the Monday sales meeting. It would mean that we do not pay our bills on that day. It would mean that on that day we do not train our children in any kind of worldly skill. It would mean that we do not do home repair. The call to the Israelites was that one day of every week they would deliberately cease from their labors and enjoy the world as they found it while learning the words of God."

It's true. There is no less a need to do this today than there was then. We must make our time with God a priority.

How can we do this? J.I. Packer notes, "Not by a frenzied rushing to pack a quart of activity into a pint pot of time (a common present-day error), but by an ordered lifestyle in which, within the set rhythm of toil and rest, work and worship, due time is allotted to sleep, family, wage-earning, homemaking, prayer, recreation, and so on, so that we master time instead of being mastered by it."

Discipline your life to be faithful in corporate worship. Ask God to show you the importance of corporate worship as a unique time in which the special presence of Jesus is manifest. Determine that you will be faithful, not simply because of what you can get out of it, but because gathering together with the community of faith is a clear testimony of God's grace to the world and the people of God.

Don't allow the demands of work to crowd out the important with the urgent. The urgent is seldom important, and the important often does not seem urgent. Don't capitulate to the "tyranny of the urgent" in your life.

Renew your commitment to obey God. God has made us so we will only function properly as we obey Him. If you are willing to obey Him, you will experience rest, joy, peace, and blessing. If you will not, you will reap in your own life the fruit of your refusal: stress, weariness, confusion, and death.

Stephen Girard was a wealthy businessman in Philadelphia and had a large number of men employed. One Saturday Mr. Girard asked his employees to work the following day. One man stepped up to his desk and said, "Mr. Girard, I can't work tomorrow because it is the Lord's Day."

52

Girard said, "You do as I ordered, or else you lose your job." The man's face turned pale. He had a family to support and a widowed mother to care for. But he said, "I simply cannot work on Sunday." Girard sent him to the cashier's desk and he was paid off and fired.

For three weeks the young man tramped the streets of Philadelphia looking for work. One day a bank president asked Girard if he knew of any trustworthy person he could hire as a cashier in a new bank about to be opened. After a little thought, Girard named the man he had fired a few weeks before. Girard described him to the banker, and went on to say, "Any man who will lose his job in order to stand for the principle of sabbath observance, is a man whom you can trust with your money"— and the young man got the job!

Our great-grandfathers used to call Sunday "The Holy Sabbath." Our grandfathers referred to it as "The Sabbath." Our fathers called it "Sunday." Our present generation calls it "The weekend." Let us take seriously the admonition to remember the Sabbath day to keep it holy.

However you might choose to interpret six days, the point is this. Every time you keep the Sabbath you are affirming that there is a Creator, that the world didn't just happen, that life isn't some meaningless coincidence, but that it is infinitely meaningful and therefore each of us has a unique significance and purpose in life.

Not bad for one day a week. No wonder, then, that remembering and keeping the Sabbath is one of the Ten Commandments. No wonder that those who have it in their lives are often happier, with richer family lives, more serenity, a community of friends, and, yes, are even healthier in all dimensions of life – body, soul, and spirit.

Sabbath is not just about church. It is about contemplation of the important things in life, the things of the soul. Mordecai Kaplan wrote, "People whose religion begins and ends with worship and ritual practices are like soldiers forever maneuvering, but never getting into action." Sabbath never ends in church. It only begins there.

A Sabbath heart is what happens in us when we make room for God in life. Sabbath is what brings us to a consciousness of the divine in the human enterprise.

By ignoring the Sabbath, we turn every day of life into an average day, a routine day, a working day. We lose a sense of celebration. We forget to stop and enjoy the world as God enjoyed creation.

Happiness comes not merely (nor even primarily) by keeping the Sabbath day holy. True happiness comes from a right relationship with God, and we become children of God through faith in Jesus Christ.

Obey God and find the special blessings His day brings. Don't let Sunday become Funday. And then maybe this simple rhyme will keep us focused:

A Sunday well spent

Brings a week of content,

And strength for the toils of tomorrow.

But a Sunday profaned

Whatever is gained,

Is a certain forerunner of sorrow.

What the Early Church Fathers Said

AUGUSTINE: *But the rite of the sabbath was taught to our ancient fathers which we Christians observe spiritually so that we abstain from all servile work, that is, from all sin (for the Lord says, "Everyone who commits a sin is a slave of sin"), and we have rest in our hearts, that is, spiritual tranquility. And, however we try in this world, we shall nevertheless not arrive at the perfect rest except when we have departed this life.*

BEDE: *Under the law the people were ordered to work for six days and to rest on the seventh, [and] to plow and reap for six years and desist during the seventh, because the Lord completed the creation of the world in six days and desisted from his work on the seventh. Mystically speaking, we are counseled by all this that those who in this age devote themselves to good works for the Lord's sake, are in future led by the Lord to a sabbath, that is, to eternal rest.*

CAESARIUS OF ARLES: *Here is suggested a repose of the heart or tranquility of the mind. Lovers of strife, authors of calamities, devotees of quarrels rather than of charity, by their uneasiness they do not admit to themselves the repose of a spiritual sabbath. Men do not observe a spiritual sabbath unless they devote themselves to earthly occupations so moderately they that still engage in reading and prayer, at least frequently, if not always. Men of this kind honor the sabbath in a spiritual manner.*
(Ancient Christian Commentary on Scripture, Vol. III)

55

REFLECTION QUESTIONS

1. The word Sabbath literally means "to cease." Based on this scripture, what is God calling us to stop on the Sabbath? In your opinion, what is the ultimate purpose of the Sabbath?

2. What are some personal barriers in your life that keep you from honoring the Sabbath? What are some of your common distractions?

3. Throughout history, people have made the Sabbath a burden by making it all about the rules. What does it look like for you to have meaningful boundaries for the Sabbath without going overboard? How can you honor God with the Sabbath without becoming legalistic?

4. How do you specifically practice the Sabbath principle? What do you do to refresh your body, spirit, and soul on a weekly basis? What steps might God want you to take to live a more enjoyable, holy, and stress-free life?

6

IS HONOR STILL HONORABLE?

Honor your father and your mother (20:12)

Parental authority is indispensable to a stable society. Throughout history, nearly all civilizations have recognized this foundational truth. From the beginning, we know that God placed humankind in families and established this relational unit as the building block of society. Parents were responsible for their children, and children were to submit to the authority of their parents. This natural law finds expression in the fifth commandment of God's revealed Law.

When there is a home in which a father and a mother function together in fulfilling the responsibility to train their children in the way they should go, there is great well-being. It is in this setting that beliefs and values are transmitted from one generation to another.

As you are reading this, it is no secret that this "traditional family" unit is under attack. A variety of family forms are now offered as viable and acceptable alternatives. The family is God's design. He has established the coming together of one man and one woman in a lifelong covenant. The feminist, homosexual agenda promoting immoral associations between people of the same sex violate God's Law. And we have "no dad" families or "no-father" children as they are now called. Reproductive "rights" of women ignore the part played by fathers. This confusion and corruption is a large part of the social landscape in which we are called to obey the fifth commandment.

We often note that The Fifth Commandment is the first commandment of the ten that marks the shift away from the God-ward focus to a focus on human relationships. The first four commandments focus on our relationship to God and the last six on our relationship to others. Jewish scholars, however, tended to divide them five and five. By doing so, they included the honoring of parents under our duty to God!

It seems to me that this makes sense. How could we ever claim to honor God, whom we have not seen, if we fail to honor our parents, whom we do see? Parental authority is divinely delegated and is an integral part of our reverence we show for God.

John Wesley notes that "as religion towards God is an essential branch of universal righteousness, so righteousness towards men is an essential branch of true religion."

This is at least one reason why Jesus could summarize all the commandments by saying that we should love God and our neighbor.

The first of these six commandments directed toward our relationships to others is this fifth one, "Honor your father and your mother."

News accounts tell the tragic story of how some national youth leaders are calling for a "children's liberation movement." They demand the privilege for a child to sue his parents, to leave school when he pleases, and to handle his own finances. One book urges that children should have the right to choose their own guardians if they don't like their parents. There are revolutionary forces at work launching an attack on family life, the like of which has never been experienced before in the history of the world. But in spite of the fact that this commandment (in some places) seems to have fallen by the wayside, God's law still stands. The command to honor father and mother has never been repealed.

Synopsis. The fifth commandment calls children, sons and daughters of all ages, to love, respect, and honor their father and mother (20:12). For children, honoring parents involves obedience to their "lawful commands", as John Wesley points out (*Notes*, Exodus 20:12) and godly teachings, even as a godly father and mother are the primary instructors and interpreters of God's covenant words (Deuteronomy 4:9-10; 6:7; 11:19; 32:46). Respecting parents reflects respecting God as one's heavenly Father (see Leviticus 19:32; Proverbs 31:28) and does not include any worship of parents or ancestors.

This commandment is so important that it is one of the only commandments in the entire Bible that gives a reason for observing it: "That your life will be long on the fertile land that the LORD your God is giving you."

The fifth commandment is not merely some abstract principle. It is perhaps one of the most practical prescriptions to healthy family relationships to be found anywhere. In giving the fifth commandment, God is not merely making a statement concerning care for the elderly – He is speaking of parents. How we treat our parents is the issue at hand. There is a blessing or curse for us based on how we act toward our parents.

I think that many people read this commandment as sort of a reward. While it may be regarded as a reward, the fact remains that it is a reason: if you build a society in which children honor their parents, your society will long survive. And the corollary is a society in which children do not honor their parents is doomed to self-destruction.

The principle spoken of here has to do with giving honor. *Honor* is a weighty word. The Hebrew word *kabed* means "to be heavy." So to honor our parents is to treat them, we might say, with a ton of respect! In fact, the Greek equivalent of the Hebrew word, used in the New Testament, *timao*, extends the thought to placing a high value upon them.

But let's dig a little deeper with this truth. For us to understand this principle of honor, we must understand the concept of community. When the fifth commandment was written, the importance of community was clearly understood. Every person had a place in the community. People were known based on their family grouping, so that "Jacob ben Isaac ben Abraham" was a title to be proud of.

A person was not only known as an individual, but also whose son you were, in the case of this example. Your identity as part of the clan or family was the important thing. You as an individual was secondary. For one to survive, relationships with the larger unit of the family need to be maintained.

It has been said that "no one is an island, entire of itself." These words of John Donne, a 17th century English poet, scholar, and cleric, are true concerning our family relationships. The words are true as well concerning our larger relationships. We live in a community, as part of the whole.

Donne goes on to say, "Any man's death diminishes me, because I am involved in mankind; and therefore never send to know for whom the bell tolls; it tolls for thee." In some sense, we are all part of one another. That is why the principle of honor and respect for one another is so important, and especially as it relates to honoring our parents.

"This, then, is the sum," John Calvin wrote in summarizing this commandment, "that we should look up to those whom God has placed over us, and should treat them with honor, obedience, and gratefulness."

It's sad that in our culture, many of the best-educated parents do not believe that their children need to show them honor, since "honoring" implies an authority figure, and that is a status many modern parents reject.

In addition, there are many parents who seek to be *loved*, not *honored*, by their children. Yet have you ever noticed that neither the Ten Commandments nor the Bible anywhere commands us to love our parents? I challenge you to find it! It's not there. The Bible takes for granted the natural affection between parent and child. It seems to me that this is particularly striking since the same Bible commands us to love our neighbor, to love God, and to love the stranger.

While we are involved in a larger community, called society, there is a basic unit within the society called the family. It is in the context of the family that we must work out our most important social relationships.

The family is the place where we begin to understand how to interrelate to one another. It is the place where we seek to develop some sense of self-esteem. It is the place where we seek to learn our value as human beings, created in the image of God. The family is where we are affirmed, corrected, encouraged, praised, or criticized and ignored.

It is within the context of family relationships where we learn from authority, or the lack thereof. It is within the context of the family that we also seek to learn the importance of values. By the example of parents, whether for good or evil. every child learns what is important or destructive. We not only learn by what is said, but by what is done.

It can truly be said that the home is the birthplace for life-molding experiences – some not so beneficial while others are. It is absolutely important and essential that parents do no shirk their God-given responsibilities. If parents do not establish this framework early, the challenge becomes greater with every parental neglect.

Why is honoring parents so important? One reason is that we, as children, need it. Parents may *want* to be honored – and they should want to be – but children *need* to honor parents. A father and mother who are not honored are essentially adult peers of their children. They are not really parents.

No generation knows better than ours the terrible consequences of growing up without a father. Statistics consistently reveal that fatherless boys are far more likely to grow up and commit violent crime, mistreat women, and act out against society in every other way. We also know, statistically and practically from science, that girls who do not have a father to honor – and hopefully, to love as well – are more likely to seek the wrong men and to be promiscuous at an early age.

Sigmund Freud, the father of psychiatry and an atheist, theorized that one's attitude toward one's father largely shaped one's attitude toward God. That, coming from an atheist!

Maybe you're wondering by now how it is that we can honor our parents. What does honor and respect mean, whether in or out of the home?

Let me suggest that there are many ways.

First, to honor is to have reverence and respect for someone with due love.

Second, one who is honored is treated with kindness and is not oppressed. Proverbs 14:31 says, "Those who exploit the powerless anger their maker, while those who are kind to the poor honor God."

Third, one honors parents through obedience and not getting one's own way (Ephesians 6:1-3).

Fourth, one who honors parents is not contemptible, quick, nor sharp to them, nor does one despise them (Exodus 21:15; Proverbs 15:5). I pastored for several years in two Southern states. It was then and still is quite common to hear children respond to questions from their parents with a "Yes, sir," or a "No, ma'am." While this may be nothing more than custom and may not represent the actual heart attitude, it is still to be preferred to the disrespectful responses of so many children and youth. To respect our parents means speaking kindly to them and about them.

Fifth, to mock one's parents, whether by actions, looks, or words, is not to honor them. Proverbs 30:17 has a strong word: "An eye that mocks a father and rejects obedience to a mother, may the ravens of the river valley peck it out, and the eagle's young eat it."

Sixth, to honor one's parents means that one should seek to make them happy. Proverbs 23:24, 25 reminds us, "The father of the righteous will be very happy; the one who gives life to the wise will rejoice. Your father and your mother will rejoice; she who gave you birth will be happy."

And *finally*, honoring one's parents means to provide for their needs, to care for them, even as they get older.

The general rule is this: they get special treatment. Parents are unique; so they must be treated in a unique way. You don't talk to them in quite the same way you do anyone else. You don't call them by their first name. You don't use expletives when referring to them or talking to them. And when you leave their home and make your own, you maintain contact with them. Having no contact with parents is the opposite of honoring them.

And yes, it is sadly but absolutely true that we all recognize and know of some parents who behave so cruelly – and I mean cruelly, not just annoyingly – that one finds it morally impossible to honor them. Cruelty, abuse and neglect are morally reprehensible and must always be condemned in the strongest way. It is never acceptable at any time in any way to act in devilish and demonic and destructive ways. Paul reminded his readers that their obedience to their parents was "in the Lord" (Ephesians 6:1). Parents' authority is not universal; they may only require obedience in such things as fit within the framework of the Lord's authority. There are such cases that exist all around us. But, thankfully, they are more rare and are the exception as compared to the multitude who are wholesome, uplifting, loving and responsible.

And remember this, if your children see you honor your parents, no matter how difficult it may sometimes be, the chances are far greater that they will honor you.

The promise of God is "that your days may be long." One aspect of the promise is that the children were to obey the teachings of God taught them by their parents so that they might live in the land and receive the blessings of God throughout life.

The primary teaching here is that if Israel would keep the fifth commandment, the nation would dwell in Canaan without interruption — but if Israel's homes were ruined by disobedient children — then, neither strong armies nor walled cities could stop the enemy.

By way of application today, if children do not obey the biblical instruction of parents, they will not appropriate the blessings of those divine truths. This promise is not categorized, or given to individuals. It is rather a general promise given to the society that adopts the principle. The principle in the promise is this: Children who are taught to obey God by honoring their parents will grow up to be responsible citizens. And responsible citizens make for a strong nation.

The second side to the promise is that the parents should communicate to their children what they have learned through their experience, so that their children's lives might be good and prolonged as they obey and follow the advice, instructions and warnings of their parents. As parents share the things of the Lord, and children do them, their lives will be blessed by the Lord, who protects and prolongs life.

I remember some years ago hearing Dr. James Dobson speak about parenting and he explained parental responsibility in a way that I will never forget. He said children walk through life like walking the hallways of school. And as they walk the hallways of life, there are many doors. Some say academics and athletics and music and clubs and church and love and friendship. Others say drugs and promiscuity and alcohol and gangs and the occult. Dobson said parents have the responsibility to lock some of those doors. Parents have the responsibility to keep some of those doors shut. Parents are called by God to be a holy and righteous pain in the aspirations of children inclined to make bad choices

We learn to honor God by honoring our father and mother. As we honor God, God honors us. We honor God because He is God. And when we give honor, we receive honor.

The day we embrace this commandment marks the beginning of honest-to-God relationships in the family.

The implication of this promise involves not only this life, but the life to come.

Honor the honorable!

What the Early Church Fathers Said

ORIGEN: *And God said, "Honor your father and your mother," teaching that the child should pay the honor which is due to his parents. Of this honor to parents one part was to share with them the necessities of life, such as food and clothing, and if there was any other thing in which it was possible for them to show favor toward their own parents.*

AMBROSE: *The formation of the children then is the prerogative of the parents. Therefore honor your father, that he may bless you. Let the godly man honor his father out of gratitude and the ingrate do so on account of fear. Even if the father is poor and does not have plenty of resources to leave to his sons, still he has the heritage of the final blessing with which he may bestow the wealth of sanctification on his descendants. And it is a far greater thing to be blessed than it is to be rich.*

(Ancient Christian Commentary on Scripture, Vol. III)

REFLECTION QUESTIONS

1. This commandment is about honoring father and mother. In what ways can and should you honor your parents? What about older parents? (Ephesians 6:1-3, 1 Timothy 5:3-8)

2. In what ways do you think we can dishonor our parents? (e.g. Exodus 21:15, 17; Mark 7:9-13)

3. Based on your experience, what kinds of things or people often receive honor in our culture? How does this align with God's design for how we ought to show honor?

4. Does honoring your parents mean obeying them no matter what they want? Explain why you feel the way you do.

5. This is the only commandment of the ten with a promise attached (see also Deuteronomy 5:16, 29, 33). What do you think is the meaning and extent of that promise? How might this apply to us today?

7

BLOOD ON OUR HANDS

Do not murder (20:13)

Human life is a deep mystery. Each cell that forms the various parts of the body has within it secrets which the powers of man cannot unlock. Even great scientists cannot tell us what life is. When we look at the reddish form of a tiny baby, and see its many functions operating perfectly, all we can do is gaze in amazement. We see life.

No one needs to be reminded of the violence in our culture. We are living in a culture that values human life less and less. We are losing, if we have not already lost, a deep and sacred sense of the critical value of human life and too many make crucial decisions without regard to consequences.

Synopsis. The sixth commandment prohibits premeditated and other unlawful killing (Exodus 20:13; see Deuteronomy 19:11-13). The prohibition here does not include accidental killing (see Deuteronomy 19:4-7), killing in war, or judicial execution.

This commandment has become – rivaled only by the seventh – the most controversial of the ten. For these are the days when it is intellectually fashionable and politically correct to rationalize all the ways that we're increasingly killing off the human race.

When we get around to this commandment, there is always a lot of talk about capital punishment, war, euthanasia, abortion, AIDS, and so on. Christians and non-Christians alike have become hotly embroiled in legal and political squabbles over these issues. We want to know how we are supposed to respond to these issues as a Christian.

Actually, the sixth commandment of the Decalogue is very short in length. It is just two words in Hebrew which are translated most properly in English as, "Do not murder." The Hebrew word clearly here refers to "murder" and signified malicious and unlawful killing. So, the word "murder" is more accurately used than the word "kill," as is used in some Bible translations. The distinction is important. Killing is unintentional. Murder is intentional.

In its context and interpretation, what this commandment has in view is the taking of life for capricious reasons – matters relating to issues of private morality, not corporate justice.

To understand what is behind this command we must reassert the value and sanctity of human life from God's perspective rather than the viewpoint, which culture has adopted, that those who do not contribute are easily expendable. Fundamental to this sixth commandment, as with all the commandments, is the existence of a personal Creator God.

God is the author of life. He formed man's body out of the dust of the ground and breathed into his nostrils the breath of life, "and man became a living soul." Job says, "God's spirit made me; the Almighty's breath enlivens me" (Job 33:4).

This commandment rests on the principle that human life is sacred – first, because it is God's gift and second, because we all bear the image of God. Human life is the most precious and sacred thing in the world. Life is not a cosmic accident that came about by chance, random processes; it is the supernatural work of God. Each human therefore has

69

inherent value and dignity. To end it, or direct its ending, is God's prerogative. Therefore, to destroy life is not only a sin against another human being, it is also a sin against God. We honor God by respecting His image in each of us, which means that we further and preserve each other's welfare at all times. This life-honoring ethos lies behind the command, "You shall not murder."

Only a firm set of principles, expressive of a biblical worldview, provides an adequate reason to value life. This then provides the foundational basis for exalting the sanctity of life and seeking to correct those who would devalue human existence.

Unfortunately, since humankind is hostile to the authority of God and His truth about life, we flagrantly violate this commandment. There are several things, not always called murder, which this commandment also clearly forbids in its broader context of Scripture that must be understood and considered.

It forbids *malice and hatred.* This has often been called "the hidden homicide." It is the desire to diminish someone or, as we say, "see them dead." It is wishing a person harm or evil or misfortune.

It is apparent from Jesus's clarification of the sixth commandment that any person can be guilty of violating it. Jesus reveals that attitudes can be as harmful as our actions (Matthew 5:21, 22). Indeed, we can say that attitudes precede actions. Jesus indicated that anger and malice in the heart (the seat of our thoughts) makes us just as guilty as actually doing it. Hate in the heart can be as much murder or violence against the person as acting it out in a physical way.

Clarence Darrow said one time, "I've never killed a man, but I've read some obituaries with a kind of sense of glee." We have the ability to harbor thoughts and feelings that are as foul as murder itself. We kill people all the time with contemptuous anger, animosity and malice, as well as hostility and gossip. They are simply little hidden murders. Sin is sin. Abortion kills. So does gossip. Murder is lethal. So is hatred. If this has been our experience, we must, without debate, engage in some deep repentance, and shed some bitter tears.

This command forbids *cruelty or violence*. Any deed which tends to injure, maim, or shorten human life is forbidden by this commandment. It is quite grievous to see how crimes against the person – muggings, knifings, shootings, bombings, and all acts of bodily assault – continue to increase in society.

This commandment forbids *abortion on demand*. Abortion is a national disgrace. In the United States, the *Guttmacher Institute* (as of July, 2020) reports that abortions are taking place at the rate of 2,362 per day, 98 per hour, 1 abortion every 96 seconds. The total number of abortions in the United States from 1973 to 2018 is 61.8+ million! The Nazi holocaust pales in statistical comparison.

The truth is that genetic science has well demonstrated that the child in the womb is "from the moment of human conception a human being in the process of arriving." The fact that for several months it cannot survive outside the womb does not at all affect its right to the same protection that other human beings merit and which will itself merit after birth. The beginning of life is not a scientific matter alone; it is a moral matter.

Murdering the unborn child is evil and sinful and is forbidden by God. For those who personally faced the choice of abortion in their own lives, God is as merciful in relation to that sin as He is to all others when we seek salvation and forgiveness through Jesus Christ!

Another increasingly acceptable form of murder is *euthanasia*, sometimes known as "mercy killing." Euthanasia speaks of gently releasing the bonds of life, especially for older people who might not be able to get well again. The purpose is to ease them out of their miserable existence.

One doctor says, "I maintain that to take the life of those who are incurably ill, is being compassionate, intelligent, and humane." Some reason (like this doctor) that when a person becomes so sick that life is almost intolerable, it is an act of mercy to kindly and humanely take that life by inducing death. This sort of reasoning appeals to the emotions, and it might seem reasonable, but it is still a transgression of God's law. The doctor who practices euthanasia is actually placing himself in the position of "playing God"— and he himself is determining when it is a person's time to die.

As Christians, we must clearly understand that all life, whatever quality it has, belongs to God. He is both the giver and the taker of life. We must not turn our minds and souls over to the Destroyer.

Another serious problem today (related to murder) is *suicide*. At its basic root, suicide is self-murder. It is perhaps one of the most desperate acts that can ever be committed. It involves running away from life and taking one's own life, for whatever desperate reason. Fundamentally, it is really usurping a right that belongs to God alone. It usurps the plan and purpose of God in our lives. It is the ultimate expression of futility.

But it should also be considered that, undoubtedly, some take their lives while suffering from some form of deep and desperate mental instability or illness - even insanity. The psyche of the mind is incredibly difficult to understand and can truly cause reckless and obsessive havoc, even to the point of death. Whatever else we might say or think about suicide, as a starting point, we must know and believe that God is merciful to those who, because of some desperate mental lapse, commit such an act.

In my ministry, I have been the pastor to families who have grieved deeply and experienced unexplainable sorrow because of a suicide in the family. It is a difficult journey and one with no easy answers. Surely it saddens us, as people of compassion, to see someone in such hopelessness and despair that he or she would rather choose suicide than live another moment. Suicide is not what God wants for anyone. Our only true relief is found in Christ. Despairing of life is a general human problem, and each of us must draw near to God in faith and hope that He will help us through the difficulties of life.

Let us return to where we started in this discussion - murder is the willful taking of human life. Whether through abortionists, child-batterers, professional thugs, amateur hit men, pre-meditated acts, or random acts, taking a human life is the ultimate expression of the fathomless wells of rage and hatred in the human heart and brings fearful results. Furthermore, it violates God's clear command.

John Wesley noted about this command, "Thou shalt not do any thing hurtful to the health or life of your own body, or any other's. This does not forbid our own necessary defense, or the magistrates putting offenders to death; but it forbids all malice and hatred to any, for he that "hateth his brother is a murderer."

What should we do about all this? There are several things to keep in mind.

First, we must have a high regard for the sanctity and dignity of all human life. Hold life in high esteem. Stated positively the sixth commandment would read, "You shall value and honor human life."

The sacredness of life means far more to us than merely prohibiting murder. It means that we seek to save the lives of those who are in danger of death, those whose lives we can spare. It means, as many Christians have grasped, that we cannot stand idly by without attempting to stop abortion on demand. It means, just as much, that when people are dying of starvation, disease, or natural disaster, we are obligated to do everything within our means to save their lives. It means that those who are political refugees, whose lives are in danger in foreign countries, may need to be allowed to find sanctuary in a country where freedom is offered and secured so that their lives can be spared.

When I care enough about something to want to save it rather than to end it, I have come to the real meaning of life and creation. "The salvation of humankind," Solzhenitsyn wrote, "lies only in making everything the concern of all."

The life that we fail to enable and sustain we condemn to death. And all the time we think that this is a commandment that has nothing to do with us.

Ultimately, the sacredness of life underscores the urgency and priority of evangelism. Jesus said, "Don't be afraid of those who kill the body but can't kill the soul. Instead, be afraid of the one who can destroy both body and soul in hell" (Matthew 10:28).

Death is a terrible thing, especially when it plunges one into a Christ-less eternity. If death is something which we are commanded to prevent if at all possible, then surely the greater evil, to be prevented as a matter of highest urgency, is that of one entering into eternity without Jesus Christ and the salvation He offers to any who will trust in Him. We must proclaim deliverance from sin through the good news of the gospel.

Second, we must restrain anger. Jesus warned that unjustifiable anger is potential murder. In reality, murder begins in the heart of a person with envy, hate, vindictiveness, or prejudice. Any of these may lead to slander, false accusation, cursing. The next step is warily and dangerously the actual deed of murder. Anger in the heart of a person cannot be allowed to hatch into vindictive speech or vicious acts.

Moses slew an Egyptian who was smiting an Israelite, yet we know he wrote the first five books of the Bible. King David, after taking Bathsheba, ordered her husband placed in a spot in battle where he would surely be killed, yet David, called a man after God's own heart, wrote many psalms in Holy Scripture. The Apostle Paul confessed that he voted for the death of the early followers of Christ, calling himself a persecutor and the chief of sinners, yet Paul was a fervent evangelist of salvation in Christ, and wrote at least thirteen books of the New Testament. This reminds us that there are redemptive stories even in the face of heinous crimes or despicable deeds committed against others.

The commandment, "Do not murder" has wide implications. Each of us needs to ask the question, "How am I living?" Am I dissipating my own life by careless habits? Am I helping to shorten the life of another? Am I harboring hatred which someday could lead to serious outward acts of violence?

The eventual answer to violence and anger and murder, is a new nature implanted by the Holy Spirit through the new birth (Romans 5:1, 5). The ultimate corrective for strife and hatred and violence, is a new respect for human life, and a

75

genuine love for other persons — and that comes through submitting our wills to the will of Jesus Christ (Hebrews 13:20-21).

What, then? The clear message of the gospel is that murder, as evil, heinous, and destructive a crime as it is, is forgivable through the grace of God, the blood of Jesus Christ, and the work of the Holy Spirit.

Only restraining and renewing grace enables anyone to keep the sixth commandment.

What the Early Church Fathers Said

CHRYSOSTOM: *How was it then when he said, "You shall not kill," that he did not add, "because murder is a wicked thing?" The reason was that conscience had already taught this beforehand. He speaks thus, as if to those who know and understand the point.*

AUGUSTINE: *"What about the prohibition, 'You shall not kill,' which is also there? If killing is evil in every respect, how will the just who, in obedience to a law, have killed many, be excused from this charge?" The answer to this question is that he does not kill who is the executor of a just command.*

(Ancient Christian Commentary on Scripture, Vol. III)

REFLECTION QUESTIONS

1. "A person's days are determined; you [God] have decreed the number of his months and have set limits he cannot exceed" (Job 14:5). All life is sacred. The moment we start saying, "This life has value, that life doesn't have value, this life does, that one doesn't," we are on a slippery slope. How does the command to not murder apply to issues like abortion, suicide, or active euthanasia?

2. What are some destructive things you have said in the past month, either out of anger or with the intent to hurt someone's reputation? When are you most tempted to speak poorly of others and "assassinate" their character?

3. What is the intended depth of this command? (see Matthew 5:21-22). How are we to handle murderous thoughts when they arise?

4. Murder begins with unresolved anger. Based on Jesus' teaching in Matthew 5:23–24, relational harmony is so important that we should interrupt our worship of God to make things right. In your own life, where do you need reconciliation? What can you do to make things right?

8

Is The Grass Greener?

Do not commit adultery (20:14)

In the *Journal of Research in Personality*, an article by Buss and Shackelford noted that it is estimated that roughly 30% to 60% of all married individuals (in the United States) will engage in infidelity at some point during their marriage. And these numbers are probably on the conservative side, if you consider that close to half of all marriages end in divorce (people are more likely to stray as relationships fall apart). According to the *Journal of Couple and Relationship Therapy*, approximately 50 percent of married women and 60 percent of married men will have an extramarital affair at some time in their marriage. That is a disturbing and alarming statistic!

As many as 65 percent of men and 55 percent of women will have an extramarital affair by the time they are 40, according to the *Journal of Psychology and Christianity*.

In Dave Carder's and Duncan Jaenicke's book, *Torn Asunder: Recovering from Extramarital Affairs*, Carder notes that adultery and divorce rates in the evangelical population are nearly the same as the general population in the United States.

Josh McDowell, who has done extensive studies of Christian youth in the area of sexual purity, states that his surveys reveal that even among youth in evangelical churches in America, forty-three percent say they have become sexually active before the age of eighteen.

Enter the seventh commandment. It reminds us that the intimacy of sexuality is to be shared within the exclusive context of providentially ordered marriage. Marriage is not an accidental but a purposeful essential element of creation. It is a divine institution providing the cornerstone of civil society.

What the words of the seventh commandment call us to face is, first, that sex is for marriage, and for marriage only; second, that marriage must be seen as a relation of lifelong fidelity; third, that other people's marriages must not be interfered with by sexual intrusion. Marriage is not a convention to be adopted as a humanly devised experiment. Nor is it a consequence to be absorbed.

Synopsis. The seventh commandment prohibits extramarital sex (Exodus 20:14). In stark contrast to some other ancient societies, the prohibition binds God's people to fidelity within a monogamous marriage. Marital unfaithfulness embodies an unfaithful relationship with God, while faithfulness in marriage embodies covenant-keeping with God.

The seventh commandment is simple, "Do not commit adultery." To our secular, pagan, and post-Christian society, this commandment is the least popular of God's laws, a quaint vestige of an ancient time, an irrelevant and out-of-date prohibition that restricts our freedom and denies us the pursuit of happiness.

John Wesley stated it simply, "This commandment forbids all acts of uncleanness, with all those desires which produce those acts and war against the soul."

The seventh commandment is written negatively, as a prohibition, in order to call our attention to a great positive truth: the importance of remaining pure and faithful before marriage and in marriage.

Why is this so important? From a biblical perspective,

the husband-wife relationship is God's chosen analogy of the kind of intimacy He desires to have with us. It is a picture of how He will love us eternally. God hates adultery because it mars and distorts the beauty of what models His relationship with us.

God's commandment against adultery also shows us something about *the importance and sanctity of marriage*, something which by any objective standard has fallen on hard times in our day.

Despite what you may have heard, God is *not* anti-sex. The Bible is *not* anti-sex. Christianity is *not* anti-sex. But sex *is* intended solely for within the confines of marriage, between a husband and a wife alone.

The sexual relationship should be associated with beautiful words like love, marriage, companionship, home, and children. Too often it is linked with rape, lust, infidelity, prostitution, pornography, and venereal disease – to name just a few.

The lawless person thinks "the grass is greener" on the other side of relationships. Sinful indulgence, unrestrained passions, and reckless living turn the "greener grass" into a cesspool of filth.

Why does God take marriage so seriously? Any number of things could be said in answer to this question. One could point to the many societal ills and the damage that is done by sexual immorality and divorce. The breakdown of the family has taken a truly staggering toll on our society.

But there is also another answer to that question that you might not have considered: Marriage is a picture of the gospel of Christ!

In Ephesians 5:21-33 the Apostle Paul has a *lot* to say about God's design for marriage. And he bases everything that he has to say about marriage on Genesis 2 (*i.e.* God's original instituting of marriage).

But in Ephesians 5:32, the Apostle Paul says something remarkable – he sums up everything that he says about husbands and wives by saying, "Marriage is a significant allegory, and I'm *applying it to Christ and the church*" (italics added).

In his commentary on the book of *Ephesians*, James Boice writes, "When God created marriage it was not simply that God considered marriage to be a good idea, though it certainly is that, or even because God thought it would be a good way to have and rear children. God created marriage to illustrate the relationship between Christ and the church."

Simply put, marriage between a husband and wife – a man and a woman – is a picture of the relationship between the Lord Jesus Christ and His Church (i.e. His redeemed people). The pattern for the husband wife is clear. The husband is to love his wife sacrificially, protecting and cherishing her; and the wife is to love, honor and obey her husband. In the privacy and sanctity of marriage there is comfort and safety. No wonder God takes marriage (and the sin of adultery which violates it) so seriously! And no wonder we should do so as well! It's about faithfulness or fidelity in relationships. Faithfulness (fidelity) in marriage is vital to its well-being.

Richard Foster, in his book *Money, Sex, and Power,* brings this into focus. "Fidelity means directing genital sex into its God-given challenge in the covenant of marriage . . . Fidelity means an enduring commitment to the well-being and growth of each other . . . Fidelity means mutuality . . . Fidelity means honesty and transparency with each other . . . Fidelity means to explore the interior world of the spiritual life together."

Having said that, we should take note more closely about what is forbidden by this commandment.

As used in this case, adultery, by strict definition, is the sin of a married person having a sexual relationship with someone other than one's spouse. Jesus did not make light of adultery in this sense, nor do the Epistles which frequently list it in their catalog of sins (Galatians 5:19; 1 Corinthians 6:9). There are Proverbs that warn against involvement with the "strange" or "other" woman (Proverbs 2:16-19; 6:26-29). But God's intention goes far beyond this aspect of the commandment.

It follows also that casual sex outside marriage (called "adultery" if either partner is married, "fornication" if not) cannot fulfill God's ideal, for it lacks the context of pledged fidelity. In casual sex, a man does not strictly *love* a woman, but *uses* and so *abuses* her (however willing she may be) and vice versa.

And the relationships intended are heterosexual only; God forbids and condemns homosexual practices (e.g., Leviticus 18:22; Romans 1:24-26ff.; 1 Corinthians 6:9-11). The first chapter of the Jewish and Christian scriptures tells us that humanity is uniquely created to show forth the image of God in the world — to make visible the invisible. God does this not just in generic, androgynous humanity, but through two very similar but distinct types of humans: male and female. They are human universals, not cultural constructs.

Some claim Jesus never said anything about homosexuality and therefore is neutral on the topic. Not true. Jesus was unequivocal in saying that to understand marriage and the sexual union, we must go back to the beginning and see how God created humanity and to what end. (See Matthew 19 and Mark 10) Jesus holds up the creation story in Genesis not as a quaint Sunday school lesson, but as authoritative — reminding us that God created each of us male and female, each for the other. And the sexual union that God created and ordains is for husband and wife to come together in physical union, one flesh. God's plan does not involve two men or two women, but one male and one female. Homosexual deeds must ever be judged in the light of the Bible – not cultural mores.

God's plan restricts sex to marriage. As noted, God's Word calls sex outside of marriage, fornication – and it is one of the sins Jesus condemned (Mark 7:21). Biblical condemnation of premarital sexual relationships should be enough for anyone who wants to live in accordance with God's Word.

So, if you are a single person, whether young or old, God requires that you flee fornication and all other sexual sin. God wants you to be both godly and guilt-free.

If there is a plan for marriage in your future, God wants you to be able to experience no regrets on your wedding day. If not, God expects you to remain sexually abstinent for life.

In a broader context and principled application of Scripture, we can also note that the seventh commandment prohibits every type of sin which invades the sanctum of sex. Our society spins out propaganda that the real fun and pleasure is found in unrestricted, unbridled promiscuity, feeding fleshly appetites in cheap and sleazy ways – this is viewed as the "greener grass."

In the jungle of modern permissiveness, the meaning and purpose of sex is missed and its glory is lost.

83

The playboy philosophy of sex partners, sexual exploitation of women, sexual affairs, unwed teenage access to contraceptives, and solving pregnancies by abortion on demand serve to remind us that the multitudes bow to the shrine of sex. The playboy attitude perverts true love which is other-person centered and degrades personality by treating persons as mere things to be used for self-gratification.

Disregard for the marriage relationship, exploitation of the partnership, narcissistic victimization of another – sexually, emotionally, psychologically – for the sake of self is a violation of the seventh commandment. It is sexual abuse of the worst kind.

Our benighted society urgently needs recalled to the noble and ennobling view of sex that Scripture clearly upholds and the seventh commandment assumes.

In the teachings of Jesus, we see that none of us escape from being included in His teaching on God's standards of sexuality and marriage. Jesus Himself taught a sexual and marital ethic that more clearly and strictly emphasized God's original plan for pure monogamous heterosexual relationships alone. Nothing else was valid — not even lustful thoughts in any other direction.

The rank and debauched emphasis on dirty or suggestive jokes, near nudity, pornography and filthy literature so easily available in our culture shows that fallen humanity's imagination is only evil continually (Genesis 6:5) and that its eyes are full of adultery that cannot cease from sin (2 Peter 2:14).

Jesus, in fact, took the commandment against adultery from the realm of the overt act to the inner thought. "But I say to you that every man who looks at a woman lustfully has already committed adultery in his heart" (Matthew 5:28).

While it is natural to admire beauty, the impulse to lust through looking and harboring lustful intent is cherishing sinful desire.

The seventh commandment lets us know that God's purposeful plan in a married relationship is a covenant that is uncompromising and absolute. God hates adultery because it defies God, defiles marriage, disregards faithfulness, destroys families, and degrades love.

Adultery is a bad thing to be avoided because marriage is a good thing worth protecting. Adultery makes ugly something that God created to be beautiful. Marriage is designed to be a permanent relationship of love and faithfulness and integrity – in every dimension, because God is the one who joins it together. "Therefore, humans must not pull apart what God has put together" (Mark 10:9).

"Do not commit adultery" is the word that calls us to truly care about the husband or wife we say we love. Not to use them. Not to exploit them. Not to ignore them. Not to patronize them. Not to manipulate them for the sake of our own satisfaction. People are not toys or trophies to be collected and abandoned. The husband or wife we love are those to whom we commit our lives, entrust our futures, and share our selves so that we can grow into fully loving spouses. In this relationship, two equals are meant to become more together than they ever could be alone.

That is the intimacy that cannot be compromised or violated – that cannot be abused – if we ourselves are ever really to become whole.

What do we do? It may serve us well to look at some practical suggestions designed to help us avoid falling into the trap of sexual sin or thinking the "grass is greener" on the other side of the fence that God has built for our safety. All of us should want to know how to safeguard our own marriages. All of us should be interested in how to avoid becoming involved in relationships that are doomed to fail.

Let me suggest as a beginning point that we center our life and relationships on Jesus Christ. The best defense is a good offense. As we aggressively follow Christ, we will be strengthening our defenses against all sin. When Jesus becomes the center of our lives, His desires will become more important than our desires.

And if you are single, determine to marry only another Christian. The Bible warns us of the dangers of yoking with an unbeliever (2 Corinthians 6:14). Do not be deceived into thinking that everything will work out because you "really love each other" or because your future spouse will "become a Christian soon," or because you are "mature enough to handle it." When it falls apart, you will pay an enormous price. Don't do it.

Marriage relationships should make spiritual growth a priority. Seek practical help from the Bible. Seek out Christians you respect and find out their secrets to happiness. Let God mold you into a spiritual person and spouse.

Focus on ways to communicate with each other. Philippians 2:4 says, "Instead of each person watching out for their own good, watch out for what is better for others." Physical and emotional fulfillment of the marriage relationship will depend greatly on the success of communication with one another in the marriage. Make your spouse a priority. Continue your courtship – remember that romance does not end with an "I do."

Meet your partner's needs – physically, emotionally and spiritually. If this is done, there will be no desire to look elsewhere for "greener grass." If we love our spouse, we should desire to fulfill one another's needs.

To see what a priority it is in the Bible, read the Song of Solomon. We must, with great sensitivity and careful communication, attempt to know the legitimate needs of our spouse. At the same time, we must be willing to give of ourselves in order to meet those needs. Proverbs 5:18,19 says, "May your spring be blessed. Rejoice in the wife of your youth. . . always be drunk on her love."

Avoid relationships that might tempt you to stray. Be sexually pure before marriage so you will not have later regrets, hurts, and comparisons. Avoid intimate situations with those to whom you might be attracted and would compromise your marriage relationship. The Bible exhorts us to flee temptation: "Run away from adolescent cravings. Instead, pursue righteousness, faith, love, and peace together with those who confess the Lord with a clean heart" (2 Timothy 2:22).

When we follow the seventh commandment, we are not just protecting ourselves, we are also protecting our relationship with our spouse, or our future spouse if we are not married. We are protecting our families. We are protecting our relationship with God. We are protecting the other person. We are protecting their spouse, their family, and their relationship.

One final word should be noted here for those who are reading this and need to hear it. Sexual sin or fornication is not the unpardonable sin. Adultery is not the unforgivable sin.

This doesn't mean that we can just commit adultery all we want though, for remember that even though God forgives us of this sin, there are long-term and devastating consequences to adultery which can affect our lives, our family, our finances, our health, and our emotional and spiritual well-being. Adultery is so destructive and damaging for the real joy and pleasure God wants us to experience in life.

If you have committed adultery, do not think that God has rejected you. He has not. He loves you, accepts you, and forgives you. Please know that God's grace is bigger than your guilt and sin. If you are willing to bring your sin to Jesus, He is willing to forgive you (1 John 1:9).

But at the same time, healthy and loving relationships are achieved only in the way God designed them: when they are between two people – a man and a woman - who love each other and are committed to each other no matter what. This is the sort of relationship God wants for you if you will let Him lead you toward it.

"Chains do not hold a marriage together," Simone Signoret wrote. "It is threads, hundreds of tiny threads, which sew people together through the years." It's weaving those threads that counts.

Relationships are not made out of service. They are made out of mutual respect and love and faithfulness. As Joe Murray puts it, "Marriage should be a duet – when one sings, the other claps."

Only God can grant us all the power we need to live with clean hands and a pure heart before Him. Only God can give us the grace to affair-proof our marriage and to keep our pleasure undefiled. Only God can give those who are single the grace to keep pure from this day forward and flee fornication. Commit yourself to obey God's seventh commandment.

What the Early Church Fathers Said

JOHN CASSIAN: *It is written in the law, "You shall not commit fornication." This is required in a beneficial way according to the simple sound of the letter by the person who is still entangled in the passions of fleshly impurity. It is necessarily observed in spiritual fashion, however, by one who has already left behind his filthy behavior and impure disposition, so that he also rejects not only all idolatrous ceremonies but also every superstition of the Gentiles and the observance of auguries and omens and of all signs and days and times. And he is certainly not engaged in divination of particular words or names, which befouls the wholesomeness of our faith.*

GREGORY THE GREAT: *The law suppressed physical sins, but our Redeemer condemned even unlawful thoughts. And so "if they do not hear Moses and the prophets, neither will they believe one who rises from the dead." When all those who neglect to fulfill the less important commandments of the law be strong enough to obey our Savior's more demanding precepts? This much is clear: anyone whose sayings they decline to fulfill, they have refused to believe.*

(Ancient Christian Commentary on Scripture, Vol. III)

THE SHEPHERD OF HERMAS: *I charge you to guard your chastity, and let no thought enter your heart of another man's wife, or of fornication, or of similar iniquities; for by doing this you commit a great sin. But if you always remember your own wife, you will never sin. For if this thought enter your heart, then you will sin; and if, in like manner, you think other wicked thoughts, you commit sin. For this thought is great sin in a servant of God. But if any one commit this wicked deed, he works death for himself. Attend, therefore, and refrain from this thought; for where purity dwells, there iniquity ought not to enter the heart of a righteous man.*

REFLECTION QUESTIONS

1. In your opinion, what is God's motivation in limiting sex to heterosexual relationships within the boundary of marriage?

2. How does the world's valuing of sex and sexuality clash with God's design? List at least three or four examples.

3. How should you deal with lustful, adulterous thoughts and sins? (Job 31:1, 1 Thessalonians 4:3-7, Colossians 3:1-6, 1 John 1:9)

4. Read Ephesians 5:3: "But among you there must not be even a hint of sexual immorality, or of any kind of impurity, or of greed, because these are improper for God's holy people." Why do you think sexual immorality and greed are mentioned together? How are they similar?

5. Read Matthew 5:27–28. In your opinion, why did Jesus extend this commandment? Why does He call us to a higher standard?

9

THE SIN OF STEALING

Do not steal (20:15)

We would all like not to be affected by stealing. But it affects all of us. Banks are hit and millions are lost in shoplifting each year, with the result of higher prices and higher insurance premiums for everybody.

As recently as 2019, retail crime remains one of the most serious problems facing superstores, retail chains and grocery stores. How big of a problem is it? Inventory shrinkage due to theft costs the U.S. retail industry over $45 billion each year. The average cost per shoplifting incident is $559. Robberies and burglaries in retail businesses are up 8.6% since 2016. A recent research article entitled *Employee Theft: Why do employees steal?* published by the California Restaurant Association stated that theft in the workplace is a growing problem that affects many employers. Nearly 95 percent of all businesses suffer from theft in the workplace and approximately 75 percent of all employees steal from their employers at least once. Employee theft and shoplifting together account for the largest source of property crime committed annually in the United States.

The eighth commandment says, "Do not steal" (Exodus 20:15). In Hebrew, it is interesting to note that the original intent of the eighth commandment was "Do not kidnap." That, of course, is stealing in the greatest form. Over time, however, the word expanded to mean not only kidnapping, but any form of stealing.

The morality of this command appears self-evident, but we live in a day when stealing is commonplace. Business suffers as anyone from the janitor to the president pilfers. We become skeptical of mechanics, doctors, clergy, politicians, parents, teachers – everyone. We say we are tired of being taken advantage of, being victimized, being robbed, yet many try to get away with as much as they can. They perpetuate their own demise by their avarice. In a world such as this, the eighth commandment is as fresh as the morning newspaper.

Synopsis. The eighth commandment prohibits stealing (Ex. 20:15). Petty theft does not match the severity of other crimes mentioned in the Decalogue. Therefore, Jewish scholars interpret this law as referring to stealing from God, such as the spoils of war that were dedicated to God (e.g. Achan in Joshua 7), and to kidnapping and selling the victim into slavery (see Exodus 21:16; Deuteronomy 24:7). Israel presumed that the function of this commandment was to protect the common property of the clan – the water well, the grazing land, the sheep – from being expropriated by the individual for the sake of personal profit.

The morality of the eighth commandment is rooted in creation: God created humankind to have possession of personal property. Humankind was accountable to God and was given ownership of all the plants, animals and the earth (Genesis 1:27-30). Humankind was also placed on earth to labor (Genesis 2:15). Honest labor and personal property go hand in hand. To the Israelite, all property was owned in common and the welfare of the community superseded all individual appropriations. God owned the land; they were at best only its keepers, its caretakers, its stewards. It had been "loaned" to them for the welfare of all. To deprive any member of the community of their share, to deprive them of their needs, was to sin against God.

John Wesley notes that this "command forbids us to rob ourselves of what we have, by sinful spending, or of the use and comfort of it by sinful sparing; and to rob others by invading our neighbor's rights, taking his goods, or house, or field, forcibly or clandestinely, over-reaching in bargains, not restoring what is borrowed or found, withholding just debts, rents, or wages. And which is worst of all, to rob the public in the coin or revenue, or that which is dedicated to the service of religion." *(John Wesley's Commentary on the Bible)*

Behind this eighth commandment lies the biblical view of property, namely, that ownership is stewardship. It is not God's will for us to have anything that we cannot obtain by honorable means, and the only right attitude to others' property is scrupulous concern that ownership be fully respected.

There is no doubt this principle of the commandment is both clear and commonplace. Nearly every law code in the world seeks to protect property, condemns stealing, and requires damages – restitution – in the way that Scripture does (Numbers 5:7; Proverbs 6:30, 31). Stealing, in the biblical sense, is not so much a private or personal sin as it is a social sin. To take what we do not need, to destroy what is useful to another, to deprive those in the community of their basic needs is stealing.

Thievery is almost a way of life for many with the life ethic that "you only go around once, so be sure to grab your share of the action." Deeply entrenched in the cultural norm is a web of graft, bribery, payoffs, extortion, confidence rackets and octopus crime syndicates. In a world where credit card companies charge from 12 to 21 percent interest and 3 billion people are living on less than $2.00 a day while the average CEO of a Fortune 500 company is earning over $8,500,000 annually, "You shall not steal" may be the commandment that proves what Jesus meant when He said, "It's easier for a camel to squeeze through the eye of a needle, than for a rich person to enter God's kingdom" (Matthew 19:24).

So, what is stealing? Stealing falls into two categories: active stealing and passive stealing. Active stealing aggressively, willfully, and maliciously takes what belongs to someone else. Stealing is not so much about things. Stealing is about relationships.

Embezzlement is the misuse or misappropriation of something that has been entrusted to us. Embezzlement is a violation of trust.

Robbery is the act of taking what belongs to another. Robbery is a broad definition and involves several kinds of stealing. Robbery generally takes things directly, often using superior forces (frequently involving a weapon). Stealing suggests *stealth*. A pickpocket, for example, uses stealth, as does a burglar. *Fraud* may also be included here and involves getting by deception what belongs to another. Here, the victim often gives what is stolen to the thief, thinking that doing so will be profitable. The only one who profits, however, is the thief.

Extortion gains possession of another person's property by the illicit use of authority or of force (not a weapon, however). Charging an excessive price is included here if one feels compelled to buy the product. For example, if your child were seriously ill and only one medicine could cure your child, you would be willing to pay almost anything to obtain it, even if the cost were excessive. In many parts of the world, law enforcement officers use their authority to extort funds from those who are vulnerable. If a police officer could, by false testimony alone, convict you of a crime that would imprison you, you would seek to pay the extortion fee to avoid the threatened punishment.

In the ancient Near East, *kidnapping* was considered a form of theft, probably because the individual would be kept as a slave, rather than because he or she would be ransomed.

In addition to these *active* forms of stealing, there are a variety of *passive* forms of stealing. While the thief just described wrongly took something from the possession of another, passive theft is the failure to give to another what belongs to him or is due him. For a variety of reasons, we may have in our possession what rightfully belongs to another, and yet fail or refuse to give it to him or her. While a more passive act, it is nevertheless stealing.

Passive stealing is a person's negligence which results in loss to a neighbor. Exodus 22:1-15 describes several acts of negligence which deprive a neighbor of his property, thus requiring restitution. For example, if a man's pastureland has been grazed bare, and he lets his animal loose so that it grazes on his neighbor's pasture and consumes it, the negligent person is guilty of passive stealing (Exodus 22:5).

A person's failure to return something lost to its owner is stealing. In Leviticus 6:3, the adage, "Finders keepers, losers' weepers," is heralded too commonly as simply an excuse for theft. To find what belongs to another and not return it when you know to whom it belongs, when possible, is to steal it.

Stealing is also failure to give what belongs to another. A day laborer is to be paid at the end of the day (Leviticus 19:13; Deuteronomy 24:14, 15). Failing to give a full day's wage for a full day's work is dishonest. Failing to give a full day's work for a full day's pay is stealing, as is shoddy or deceptive work. It is theft when debts are left unpaid, thus robbing the person owed of the use of money to which that person is morally entitled. Theft of time is perhaps the most common form of theft today. Starting late, finishing early, stretching coffee breaks, lunch and tea breaks, and wasting time in between is theft.

And the Bible reminds us that failing to give what belongs to God is stealing. The prophet Micah asked, "Will a man rob God?" When asked, "How do men rob God?" the prophet replied, "In tithes and offerings" (Micah 3:8). By withholding the tithe or failing to use the resources God has given us, a person is guilty of robbing God. When we fail to recognize the fact that God is Lord of our finances and that all our resources are essentially on loan from Him, we will fail to honor Him in these money matters and thus be guilty of stealing from Him.

It is possible to steal someone's reputation. Destroying someone's credit by malicious gossip behind the person's back is a form of thievery. "Who steals my purse, steals trash," wrote Shakespeare, "but he that filches from me my good name . . . makes me poor indeed." Stealing would have the thief get ahead at the expense of one's neighbor.

So, after all this, what is the corrective and the cure for stealing? For those who had stolen from another, the Old Testament prescribed restitution to those who had been defrauded. In Leviticus 6, we find that the sacrificial system provided a means for a thief to repent, to make restitution, and to obtain forgiveness. Restitution is a corrective, but not a cure for the sin of stealing. It's no less true today.

In the New Testament, Zaccheus demonstrated his repentance by restoring fourfold all the money he had wrongly and unjustly taken (Luke 19:8). Zacchaeus was applying the four-sheep-for-one-rule found in Exodus 22:10.

In the Belfast Revival of 1922-23, converted shipyard workers brought back tools and equipment they had "knocked off" in such quantities that in once place an additional storage shed had to be provided to hold the goods returned. That truly showed spiritual reality of the principle of restitution.

In the early 1980's while I was pastoring in the Northwest, a young man in the church I pastored came to Christ. Shortly after his conversion, he asked me to accompany him on a "restitution road" as he returned to retail stores where he had taken items that did not belong to him – everything from a Walmart store to a gun shop! I was with him the whole day retracing those "stealing steps" as he sought to pay for or give back what he had stolen. What freedom he experienced as he followed the biblical mandate of restitution! It was a cleansing of his guilty conscience, a clean page in the journal of his life, a fresh start, a new day.

Thievery must be overcome by repentance and faith in Christ. "Thieves should no longer steal. Instead they should go to work, using their hands to do good so that they will have something to share with whoever is in need" (Ephesians 4:28). The thief does not wish to work, but rather to live off others who do work. The thief looks upon the needy as the vulnerable, whose weakness can be well used to the thief's advantage, and thus to prey upon them.

The Christian must put away laziness and go to work. The Christian views the needs of others as the opportunity to manifest the love and grace of God to others, giving of his own resources. The things we choose to possess, the desires we have – satisfied or not – tell us who we really are. What do you buy? To whom do you give? What don't you buy? To whom do you not give?

Nothing more dramatically demonstrates the radical change which conversion – faith in Christ – produces in the life of a sinner than the change which occurs in the Christian who was formerly a thief.

So, what does all this mean? We must remember that stealing takes from others with no thought of giving in return. Justice demands that when one takes, he must give something equal in return. Christianity teaches us to give freely, with no expectation of getting something in return.

As we seek to live righteously with this commandment, we must consider what we owe our neighbors and should then pay them what we owe. And in this command, as with the others, we must be reminded that this rule was established for our hearts as well as our hands.

True repentance will be accompanied with fruit – restitution made to the victim, diligence in a legitimate vocation, and deeds of generosity. In Christ, the converted thief can then learn contentment. Do not steal. That means to meaningfully preserve fairness and justice in all relationships.

So, what must we do in light of this commandment? Three things: First, determine your treasure (Matthew 6:21), for wherever it is, there your heart is also. Second, deal with your sin. Stealing is sin. Confess it to Jesus and He will forgive you (1 John 1:9). Third, do not turn back. As Jesus said to one woman who had been caught in a sinful act, go and sin no more!

What the Early Church Fathers Said

ST. BASIL THE GREAT: *When someone steals a man's clothes we call him a thief. Should we not give the same name to one who could clothe the naked but does not? The bread in your cupboard belongs to the hungry man; the coat hanging unused in your closet belongs to the man who needs it; the shoes rotting in your closet belong to the man who has no shoes; the money which you hoard up belongs to the poor.* (From a homily on the Gospel of Luke)

CLEMENT OF ROME: *Let the strong take care of the weak; let the weak respect the strong. Let the rich man minister to the poor man; let the poor man give thanks to God that he gave him one through whom his need might be satisfied.*

ARISTIDES: *Christians love one another. They do not overlook the widow, and they save the orphan. The one who has ministers ungrudgingly to the one who does not have. When they see a stranger, they take him under their own roof and rejoice over him as a true brother, for they do not call themselves brothers according to the flesh but according to the soul.*

ST. JOHN CHRYSOSTOM: *To deprive is to take what belongs to another; for it is called deprivation when we take and keep what belongs to others. By this we are taught then when we do not show mercy, we will be punished just like those who steal. For our money is the Lord's, however we may have gathered it. If we provide for those in need, we shall obtain great plenty. This is why God has allowed you to have more, not for you to waste on prostitutes, drink, fancy food, expensive clothes, and all the other kinds of indulgence, but for you to distribute to those in need. . . for you obtained more than others have, and you have received it, not to spend it for yourself, but to become a good steward for others as well.*

REFLECTION QUESTIONS

1. This commandment is about stealing. What are some obvious ways, and subtle ways, you can steal?

2. Read Proverbs 10:2: "Wealth you get by dishonesty will do you no good, but honesty can save your life." How does this scripture speak to the old saying "The ends justifies the means"?

3. Read Job 24:16–17. Stealing happens in secret with the hope of never getting caught. How does stealing harm the thief, even if he or she isn't caught? What are the negative consequences of breaking this commandment?

4. Read Romans 2:21:"You who preach against stealing, do you steal?" In your opinion, why is it easy to justify and rationalize taking something that doesn't belong to you?

5. In your opinion, what does it mean to steal from God?

10

THE SANCTITY OF TRUTH

Do not testify falsely against your neighbor (20:16)

"What a tangled web we weave. We all practice to deceive." That was the headline of a *New York Times* article. Maybe you would be shocked to know what it reported. "Ninety-one percent confess that they regularly don't tell the truth. Twenty percent admit they can't get through a day without conscious, premeditated 'white' lies."

Brandon Gaille, in a 2017 published research article entitled *25 Nose Growing Statistics on Lying*, reported that by the age of four, 90% of children have learned the concept of lying. Gaille also reported that based on studies performed in the past, it is estimated that 60% of adults cannot have a ten-minute conversation without lying at least once. Within those ten minutes, an average of three lies were told!

Among other reasons, people lie to save face, shift blame, avoid confrontation, get one's way, to be nice, or lie to make oneself feel better.

Immeasurable harm is done by lies, slander, gossip, and abusive speech. So, along comes this ninth timeless principle and commandment that forbids inflicting injury with our tongues: "Do not testify falsely against your neighbor" (Exodus 20:16). It is repeated in Deuteronomy 5:20. The word for falsely in Exodus means "untrue," while in Deuteronomy the word means "insincere," pointing to the deceitful purpose which breeds the falsehood.

Synopsis. Specifically, the ninth commandment prohibits false testimonies in a legal setting (20:16), especially those that lead to condemnation and execution of the innocent (e.g., 1 Kings 21; see Proverbs 6:16-19). There are various factors that would lead to generating false testimony; siding with the majority, favoritism, bribery, classism, and racism or discrimination against the foreigners (Exodus 23:2-9).

The false testimony which is forbidden here is that which is given in a court of law, by which a person will be found innocent of guilty of an offense. This commandment draws attention to the witnesses in any given trial. If the testimony given during a trial were false, a just verdict would be threatened. The ninth commandment seeks to ensure a just verdict by prohibiting the bearing of false, that is, untrue testimony, which may either wrongly incriminate or justify a person who is accused of wrongdoing.

While perjury is certainly a primary consideration of this commandment, the broader and biblical principle of holding truth sacred goes beyond the court of law and touches all our living.

This commandment is a call to truthfulness, a commitment to truth that is more than skin deep. God delights in truth in the inward being. Honesty is first and foremost an affair of the heart.

John Wesley noted that this commandment "forbids speaking falsely in any matter, lying, equivocating, and in any way devising and designing to deceive our *neighbor*. Also, speaking unjustly against our neighbor to the prejudice of his reputation. And (which is the highest offense of both these kinds put together), bearing false witness against him, laying to his charge things that he knows not, either upon oath, by which the third commandment, the sixth, or eighth as well as this are broken. Or in common conversation, slandering, backbiting, tale-bearing, aggravating what is done amiss, and any way endeavoring to raise our own reputation upon the ruin of our neighbor's." *(John Wesley's Commentary on the Bible)*

What does it mean to bear false witness, or in more modern terms, to lie? To lie is to make an untrue statement with an intent to deceive or to create a false or misleading impression. A simple definition would simply be saying that which is not true with intent to deceive.

How is it that we bear false witness? There are many ways.

We bear false witness by *deception*. We all know this kind of lie. It is the kind of lie when a person gets in our face, looks us straight in the eye, maybe even wags a finger in our face, and deceives us, knowing full well the truth. This is malicious and is intended to cause harm to another person and is direct and outright deception. Along with this, the formal lie we know as perjury – a false statement under oath in court – is included.

We bear false witness by *omission*. If we are selling our home, and we list on the advertisement that it is in excellent condition, we should be truthful. If we know that the roof leaks during heavy rains, or that the stove is on its way soon to failure, and we fail to tell the buyer, we have lied. We have misrepresented the truth to them and have ruined our witness because we have lacked integrity.

We bear false witness by *insinuation*. This means we allow an untruth to go unchallenged. If we know something being said or taught is not true, we have an obligation to bring it out into the open. If we allow lies to remain lies, we participate in those lies.

We bear false witness when rumors are promoted by *gossip*. This is perhaps one of the most insidious lies. Gossip is the passing on of unverified or unnecessary information which lead to addition or subtraction of information that causes harm to someone. Sometimes we do not even realize we are lying when we do it. Just because we do not know it is a lie, however, does not make it less dishonest. We must check the facts before we tell something we heard. Not only that, we must also decide whether we even need to share it.

There is the false witness of *vain flattery*. When we tell someone a lie in order to gain favor in that person's eyes, this is still a lie. It has been said, "A flatterer is one who says things to your face that they wouldn't say behind your back." God promises to "cut off all slick-talking lips and every tongue that brags and brags" (Psalm 12:3).

There is the false witness of *slander and detraction*. Slander is wrongly imputing vice to another person, whereas detraction is groundless diminishing of another's virtue. Potiphar's wife slandered Joseph when she falsely accused him in the Old Testament story.

There is the false witness of *gossip*. "Destructive people produce conflict; gossips alienate close friends" (Proverbs 16:28). Pascal wrote, "I lay it as a fact that if all men knew what others say of them, there would not be four friends in the world." Solomon identifies the peculiar enticement to engage in gossip. "The words of gossips are like choice snacks; they go down to the inmost parts" (Proverbs 18:8).

We must learn to break the gossip chain. "One who seeks love conceals an offense, but one who repeats it divides friends" (Proverbs 17:9). Friendships are broken, relationships are ruined, and peace is destroyed through careless gossip. When you have a desire to talk about someone, ask these questions: Is it true? Is it necessary? Is it edifying? Will it help that person's image? Can I say it to the person's face? If you cannot, do not say it.

There is the false witness of *boasting*. Overstatement about self is boasting, whether about one's feats, position, salary, grades, or abilities. Or one may testify about their former wicked deeds, making others think them a worse character than they really were.

There is the false witness of *keeping quiet*. If you hear someone being defamed on information about which you have some facts to the contrary that will correct the information, it is silent participation in the lie to fail to speak out the evidence that would clear the sullied character of the victim.

There is the false witness of *half-truths*. We often call them "white lies" but the effect is still the same – the wording we give can be true but leave a wrong impression. Caution should be exercised to correctly quote the remarks of others, especially those with whom we disagree. Half-truths may come in the form of a deceptive shrug of the shoulders, emphasis on a certain portion of a sentence, tone of voice, or by a glance away when we know that the truth really is and could make a difference by letting it be known.

There is the false witness of *lies to God*. Unkept vows to God are lies. People vow to attend church regularly, serve faithfully, attend prayer meetings, but fail to keep their word to God.

While this is by no means an exhaustive list, the point should be clear – bearing false witness is a sin and it is insidious. It works its way into the social fabric of our lives and wreaks great havoc. Our society operates on a supposed foundation of truth. Lying is a profound mischief. It affects the liar and the one lied about. One lie leads to another until a person becomes tangled in the octopus of deceit.

Mark Twain put it this way: "If you tell the truth, you don't have to remember anything." How true that really is!

Lying leads others to think truth is unimportant. Lying can convict the wrong person. No one this side of judgment can measure the damage done by the slandering and gossiping tongue.

A. B. Simpson wrote, "I would rather play with forked lightning or take in my hands living wires, with their fiery currents, than speak a reckless word against any servant of Christ or idly repeat the slanderous darts which thousands of Christians are hurling on each other."

Lying affects our relationship with God. Lying is contradictory to God's nature, for He is truth. Lying, unless forgiven, will keep us from heaven.

In the end of the discussion, we need to consider the positive command that is implied in this negative. The positive is that we should seek our neighbor's good and speak truth to them and about them. When the love which seeks the good prompts us to withhold truth which, if spoken, would bring that person harm, the spirit of the ninth commandment is being observed.

What should we be doing? We should first *find repentance* for bearing false witness. We must recognize its sinfulness, which helped nail Christ to the cross, and ask Him to forgive us through His redeeming sacrifice. Then, as God's children, we will have the Holy Spirit enabling us to keep the New Testament command, "Therefore, after you have gotten rid of lying, *Each of you must tell the truth to your neighbor* because we are parts of each other in the same body" (Ephesians 4:25).

We must *establish accountability*. "Tell me if I have integrity!" Talk to people. Talk to five people and ask them this. But make sure your heart is open to hear the truth in love.

We must *meditate* on Scripture. Jesus said, "I am the truth." We need to ask, "What would Jesus do in this situation?" Think of purity and Scripture. Lying and truthfulness cannot coexist. When the Spirit comes in, He will lead you into truth. Meditate on Him.

We must consciously *tell the truth*. Work at it. Say it. When you say things, tell the truth. Keep practicing. If you make a mistake, say "I'm sorry; I was wrong." Correct it and tell the truth. Practice that.

Truth in human relationships is love. The spirit of Christ within us is to "speak the truth in love." There is health and joy in our lives when we observe truth. We worship a God of truth. Jesus came revealing truth. The Christ follower seeks to reflect it straight. We need "truth in our inward parts."

Maybe your words have been less than truthful and caused others to be hurt. Your addition of information might have added to that gossip. Replace those words of gossip with words of praise and proclamation. Replace lying with truthfulness.

Get into the habit of using your lips for praise and worship. Then, speak the truth – in love!

What the Early Church Fathers Said

AUGUSTINE: *The law says to you, for example, "You shall not bear false witness." If you know what the truth of the evidence is, you have light in your mind. But if you are overcome by greed for sordid gain and decide in your heart of hearts to bear false witness for the sake of it, then you are already beginning to be tossed about by the storm in the absence of Christ. You are being heaved up and down by the waves of your avarice, you are being endangered by the tempest of your desires, and with Christ apparently absent, you are on the verge of sinking.*

AUGUSTINE: *If anyone should argue that not every lie should be called false witness, what will he answer to this statement which is also in the sacred Scriptures: "The mouth that belies, kills the soul." If anyone should think that this passage can be interpreted to except certain lies, he may read in another passage: "You will destroy all that speak a lie." In this connection, our divine Lord said with his own lips, "Let your speech be 'yes, yes'; 'no, no'; and whatever is more comes from the evil one. Hence the apostle too, when he directs that the old man should be put off, under which term all sins are understood, goes on to explain his remark and specifically says, "Therefore put away lying and speak the truth."*

(Ancient Christian Commentary on Scripture, Vol. III)

REFLECTION QUESTIONS

1. When is it easiest for you to speak falsely about others? In your opinion, what are the similarities and differences between slander and gossip?

2. Read John 7:18: "Whoever speaks on their own does so to gain personal glory, but he who seeks the glory of the one who sent him is a man of truth; there is nothing false about him." Could the same be said about you? Are you a person of truth? What needs to change? Is there someone with whom you need to "come clean" in order to restore your integrity?

3. Read Proverbs 10:9: "The man of integrity walks securely, but he who takes crooked paths will be found out." Why are both "telling" and "living" the truth important? What is the impact of duplicity and deception in our lives?

4. Read Ephesians 4:25: "Therefore each of you must put off falsehood and speak truthfully to his neighbor, for we are all members of one body." Based on this scripture, why should we speak truthfully? What benefits have you experienced in a relationship with someone who speaks the truth?

11

NEEDY OR GREEDY?

Do not desire and try to take your neighbor's house (20:17)

I recall a cartoon in the *Saturday Review*: A corporate head is standing before the table at which the Board of Directors is seated. He states the situation: "Our days of gobbling up corporations are over. As of 10:15 this morning we've been gobbled up." Too often in this world, we are either the grabber or the grabbee. That is the not the way God planned it.

Greed. Think about it for a moment. It is rampantly promoted in our culture today. Advertisements entice us to covet. Covetousness takes the form of an excessive, inordinate desire for whatever one does not have, especially what belongs to another. Greed causes people to overindulge, to consume more than they really need, to hunger for things and pleasures which tyrannize their hearts.

The tenth commandment states: "Do not desire and try to take your neighbor's house. Do not desire and try to take your neighbor's wife, male or female servant, ox, donkey, or anything else that belongs to your neighbor" (Exodus 20:17). This commandment speaks to a basic problem in human relationships and also to our own inner experience.

At first glance, this commandment seems to be totally without substance, totally without value. After all, who can see "covetousness" and how many people would be honest about it? And we might think, since when did wanting something have any moral importance as long as we don't do anything immoral in the process of getting it?

Synopsis. The tenth commandment prohibits covetousness, one's affection turning from God to another, perhaps the root of all sinful actions. The desire to possess something or someone that belongs to another or that is prohibited can lead to breaking all other commandments. In obeying the first commandment, one submits to the rest. In breaking it, one is liable to lawlessness. In obeying the last commandment, one gains self-control and mastery over other sins. In breaking it, one can be mastered by the rest of sins.

The tenth commandment is perhaps the most revealing and devastating of all the commandments, because it deals explicitly with the inward nature of the law. Covetousness is an attitude of the inward nature which may or may not express itself in an outward acquisitive act. Since coveting cannot be witnessed and prosecuted, this prohibition addresses internal sinful motivations and desires and seeks to uproot them before they are carried out in action.

According to the *Oxford English Dictionary*, covetousness is the inordinate and culpable desire of possessing that which belongs to another or to which one has no right. So, at its root, it refers to illegitimate desire.

The tenth commandment is a commandment that clashes with our culture in so many ways.

Covetousness is the root of lawlessness. It motivates people to slander, steal, commit adultery, murder and it destroys God's worship. It is the disease of unbridled desire. It is the need to be satiated – and then to have even more. It is the need for constant satisfaction of the senses. It is the inability to be at peace with the self, with life, with necessities.

111

It is self-aggrandizement gone mad and life gone totally narcissistic.

In Colossians 3:5, Paul called coveting idolatry, because the things coveted become a person's god – controlling one's life. Covetousness is a sin of the soul, a sickness of the mind that leads to perpetual discontent.

John Wesley noted that this command "forbids all desire of doing that which will be an injury to our neighbor; this forbids all inordinate desire of having that which will be a gratification to ourselves. O that such a man's house were mine! Such a man's wife mine! Such a man's estate mine! This is certainly the language of discontent at our own lot, and envy at our neighbor's, and these are the sins principally forbidden here. God give us all to see our face in the glass of this law, and to lay our hearts under the government of it!" *(John Wesley's Commentary on the Bible)*

Some people covet relationships – another person's family, spouse, or children. Some people long to supplant someone in the affections of a wife or husband, to have the home and family they have. Some people covet the means of production that an individual has, either his ox which plows in his field, or the servants that work for him. Some people covet another person's ability to generate wealth. Some people covet someone's wealth, the things he or she owns. The desire for things that belong to our neighbor can literally destroy us – from the inside out.

It should be clear that there is nothing wrong with setting goals and working hard toward an academic degree, the purchase of a home, or a promotion at work. The idea that all desires are evil and wrong is a teaching of Buddhism, not of Christianity. The tenth commandment focuses on an unhealthy coveting of what belongs to another, and for which we are not prepared to work hard and earn, or for which we work for the wrong motivations.

If our motivation is self-focused, or even if it is to earn God's favor (which cannot be earned), then we can easily find ourselves in violation of the tenth commandment. Comparing ourselves with others and wanting something or someone we don't have can give birth to coveting. Whether it is a possession, a position, or a person, we must keep ourselves free from such inordinate desires.

The *Westminster Shorter Catechism* summarizes the instruction of the tenth commandment in this way: "The tenth commandment requires full contentment with our own condition, with a right and charitable frame of spirit toward our neighbor, and all that is his . . . . [and] forbids all discontentment with our own estate, envying or grieving at the good of our neighbor, and all inordinate notions and affections to anything that is his."

This commandment is about lust, about the insatiable need not simply to have more than we need but to have more than is good for us. Our society thrives on materialism, cashing in on the sin of covetousness. It modus operandi is to create within our hearts a longing for things we do not have. Not only a longing, but also an attitude of need and entitlement. We need it. We deserve it. And we will get it. Especially if someone else has it.

Throughout the Scriptures, we learn that coveting has certain characteristics which make it possible to identify this evil in its various forms.

Coveting is a *desire*. It is a matter of the heart, an attitude, a matter of strong emotion. As such, coveting is somewhat unique among the evils condemned by the commandments, While the other commandments deal with

113

forbidden acts, this final commandment forbids an attitude –
not an act.

Coveting is a *strong desire*. It is a motivation so strong
that the one who covets something will have it if there is any
way possible to do so, even if it involves an evil action. It is a
consuming desire and an evil attitude - which will likely lead
to an evil action.

Coveting is *excessive desire* for what one does not
have. In brief, coveting always wants more. It is not content
with what it already has, no matter how much that may be.

Coveting *wants what is forbidden*, that which belongs
to another and which cannot be rightfully and justly obtained.
The assumption in this commandment is that we covet what
we cannot have, that is, what our neighbor either cannot give
up (like his wife or his land), or what he will not give up. The
covetousness here condemned is that which wants what
another has and is clearly self-centered.

Coveting is a *deliberate desire* for which one is
responsible. In effect, the individual is held accountable for
covering the sin when convicted by the Holy Spirit and then
dealing with it. This is necessary because no other human
being can know our thoughts.

Coveting is a *well-defined desire*. It is a desire to have
a thing which belongs to a person. Greed may desire money or
material things; coveting desires our neighbor's car, house, or
wife. Coveting is well-defined and specially focused on lust.

Covetousness is a *destructive desire*. One reason
covetousness is condemned is because of its consistently
detrimental effects.

First, covetousness hinders the generosity which God
requires of us. Covetousness sees generosity as a threat to the
accumulation of things which are strongly desired.

Second, covetousness is often the motive for an offense against someone else. The person who covets another's "ox" (in whatever form it takes) is going to find a way to get it. While coveting does not always lead to other sins, sin often begins with coveting. So, the Scriptures speak of coveting as the source of many evils.

Third, covetousness is self-destructive, as the one who covets destroys himself, as well as others.

Covetousness is a *deified desire* – idolatry. The Ten Commandments began with a prohibition of idolatry, and end with a prohibition of covetousness which is called idolatry throughout the Bible.

If asked which is the least important of the Ten Commandments, most would reply the last one here. Compared to theft, adultery, and murder, how unimposing covetousness sounds. One preacher spoke on this sin of covetousness under the subject, "The Sin We Never Admit." However, a little reflection will show how crucial this commandment is.

The sin of covetousness generally leads to other violations of God's law. It destroys our walk with God. To covet first place is to deify self and set God aside, breaking the first commandment. Coveting the fame and recognition of others can lead us to taking God's name in vain. To covet time and possessions can lead us to violate God's command for a day of rest. To covet our parent's freedom can cause us to reject their authority. Coveting another person's money, property, or power can lead to murder. Coveting another person's spouse may lead to adultery; coveting property can lead to stealing and lying. See how it works? Covetousness destroys us.

Coveting destroys contentment. The more we get, the more we want. It is a vicious cycle that has no end. The truth is, things (possessions) do not satisfy.

Coveting destroys friendships. Envy creeps in so subtly and causes us more grief than we need. It is hard to be friends with someone who always wants what is yours.

Coveting destroys our financial well-being. We generally act upon our desires. When we want something that badly, normally we go out and get it. This starts a downward spiral of self-destruction.

Coveting covers up the spiritual. The more emphasis we put on "things" the less time we have to focus on God. The pursuit of material happiness becomes more important that the pursuit of holiness.

After all this, what can be presented as the cure for covetousness? Let me offer here some things that can help us.

Guard your heart. Condemn and check the first motions of the inner man toward any sinful desire. Harbor no lust of flesh, lust of eyes, or pride of life. Nip the covetous thought in the bud. Paul advised, in warning against the love of money as the root of all evil, "man of God, run away from all these things" (1 Timothy 6:11). Remember the heart is the well-spring of life from which all the issues of life flow. If the heart is right, our actions will be right.

Cultivate contentment. Discontent breeds desire. Our high standard of living in Western culture makes the luxuries of yesterday become the necessities of today. If happiness came through things, the people we know around us should be the happiest people on earth. But often, they are not. We admit our culture is stricken with people who are depressed and in despair. They have much on the outside – but little on the inside! The antidote to covetousness is contentment.

Our lives are lived between two fixed points of saying no to covetousness and learning to say yes to contentment. "Godliness with contentment is great gain," wrote Paul (1 Timothy 6:6). This involves learning to be content with what we have (Hebrews 13:5). Contentment is one dimension of happiness, which is itself the fruit of a relationship. Knowing the love of Christ is the one and only source from which true contentment ever flows.

Practice the tithe. Failure to tithe is robbing God and demonstrates that money is prized too highly. Tithing cuts the nerve of selfishness, making us giving persons rather than grabbing persons.

Enjoy your possessions with moderation. We are to trust "in God, who richly provides everything for our enjoyment" (1 Timothy 6:17). Remember, it is permissible to enjoy whatever economic surplus the Lord has given us, provided the surplus was not received either as a violation of God's law or the laws of men.

Think often of the cross of Christ. It has been said, "Covetousness hides and hoards, but the melting power of the cross, kindled in the heart, can release a believer's silver to flow in the service of the Lord."

The Christ on the cross came not to be ministered unto, but to minister, and He washed the feet of His disciples. For the joy that was set before Him, He endured the cross, and laughed at the shame. He came "that *they* might have life and have it fully." He taught us to love neighbor and to love enemy, and when we do this, envy has no place in the scheme of things.

Rather than coveting other people's goods, we should covet Jesus Christ – to know Him, to be rich in His grace, and wealthy in His Word and the Holy Spirit. Our inner longings

117

can only be satisfied in Christ. Having Him, we lack nothing. Life is accepted without discontent because He is sovereign. "The LORD will do all this for my sake" (Psalm 138:8).

The Scriptures teach, "Your way of life should be free from the love of money, and you should be content with what you have" (Hebrews 13:5). What a great liberation would be ours if we lived in such contentment! Jesus said, "It is more blessed to give than to receive" (Acts 20:35). The very idea that it is better to give what we have to others, rather than to covet for ourselves what someone else possesses, is a radical reorientation of an entire worldview that can so easily become dominated by worldly values rather than the values of the kingdom of God.

Indeed, the tenth commandment represents a reorientation of our lives around the values of contentment, recognizing the needs of those less fortunate than ourselves, and drawing our identity and self-worth from God. It returns us to that reorientation of life and heart that the Decalogue pronounced in the opening command. This is the great gift that is ours if we keep this commandment.

There is a divine covetousness to possess. "Just like a deer that craves streams of water, my whole being craves you, God" (Psalm 42:1). There is a hunger and thirst after righteousness. There is an honest yearning for God, and "the unsearchable riches of Christ" (Ephesians 3:8).

The way we deal with what we have determines the way we deal with everything else around us. It also measures the quality of our souls. Are you content today? Are you joyful with the place God has drawn for you? Are you looking to God today, or are you trying to outdo "Mr. Jones" down the road?

Many of us are tempted to find the key in *doing*, but the answer is actually found in *being*. It is vital that we are routinely humbled by the reminder that the Christian life is grounded, not in what we can *do*, but in what has been *done* for us and what we need done to us – in and through Jesus Christ.

The godly Robert Murray McCheyne, who died at the age of twenty-nine while minister at St. Peter's Church in Dundee, Scotland, wrote: "It has always been my ambition to have no plans as regards myself." It is possible, by the grace of God, to move from greed to generosity, from selfishness to the service of others. Let us forget about "the Joneses" and focus upon God.

What the Early Church Fathers Said

AMBROSE: *Love of money then is an old, ancient vice, which showed itself even at the declaration of the divine law; for a law was given to check it.*

GREGORY THE GREAT: *Old Testament law forbids anyone to lust after another man's wife, but it does not decree punishment for the king who commands his soldiers to perform dangerous feats or who desires a drink of water. We all know that David was pricked by lust and desired another man's wife and took her. The blows his sin deserved followed, and he made amends for the evil he had done by tears of repentance.*

AUGUSTINE: *The law said, "You shall not covet," in order that, when we find ourselves lying in the diseased state, we might seek the medicine of grace. By that commandment [we might] know both in what direction our endeavors should aim as we advance in our present mortal condition and to what a height it is possible to reach in the future immortality. For unless perfection could somewhat be attained, this commandment would never have been given to us.*

(Ancient Christian Commentary on Scripture, Vol. III)

REFLECTION QUESTIONS

1. Read Proverbs 19:23: "The fear of the Lord leads to life; then one rests content, untouched by trouble." In your life, how has the health of your spiritual walk influenced your levels of contentment?

2. How is coveting a form of idolatry (Colossians 3:5)?

3. What should rule our hearts instead? (Philippians 4:11-13; 1 Timothy 6:6-10; Hebrews 13:5)

4. In your own life, what drives you to have an unhealthy desire for things you don't already own? What false beliefs influence this kind of behavior? The writer also raises the idea of "more is never enough." Does this influence you – and if so, how does it influence?

5. Read Luke 3:11–14. In this passage, we see that a lack of contentment leads to extortion - abusing power to receive more. How does your personal discontentment get expressed in your life?

12

WHAT ABOUT JESUS?

There is just no way at all to get around it. None of us can look into the mirror of God's Law and feel good about ourselves. Not even for one moment. Not if we're honest. Along with everybody else, we are accountable to God. It is God's holy standard that makes us painfully aware of the reality that we are lawbreakers. While we affirm that God's commands are good, they seem to bring nothing more than a moral burden that crushes us under the weight of God's holiness. On the surface, they seem to fill us with guilt and shame and regret.

The commandments are about more than just commandments. They are about the things that make us whole in body, soul, and spirit. They are about the will of a loving God to us revealed through Jesus Christ that the love that sustains the universe should never die. They are about experiencing abundant life, rather than death.

Our difficulty with the Ten Commandments can be resolved by understanding the aim of God's Law in the context of redemptive history. When we fail to see the context in which the Law was given, we tend to overlook the relationship of the Law of God to the grace of God.

"You saw what I did to the Egyptians, and how I lifted you up on eagles' wings and brought you to me . . . I am the LORD your God who brought you out of Egypt, out of the house of slavery" (Exodus 19:4; 20:2).

These are the words of the God of Israel to Moses as he stood on Mount Sinai and looked back at what God had done for His people, how He had delivered them from slavery in Egypt. It is important to remember that when God gave the Israelites the Law, their status as God's people had already been established.

Since Israel was given a new life after God delivered them out of Egypt, the Law functioned to show Israel what this new life was to look like. And the laws given at Sinai were not arbitrary but stemmed from the character of God and His original purpose for humankind in creation.

The purpose of Israel's obedience was to reflect God's nature to the world around them as a concrete expression of their devotion to God. The same is true for Christians today; God's Law establishes a separate and unique identity for God's people.

However, the history of Israel (and our own hearts) confirm that the ideals of God's Law cannot be achieved without God's divine intervention. The Ten Commandments expose our sinful motives and behavior for what they are, namely, transgression of specific commands.

The Law of God was not given to save us. We know from experience that the Ten Commandments do not have the power to transform us or liberate us from the power of sin. So, the Law is like a teacher who shows us God's holiness, our sinfulness, and our need for salvation. God's Law was given to pinpoint sin, to define it, to bring it out of its hiding place.

Sin is an offense against God. His Law is broken by our disobedience. It is by our rebellion that we despise His authority in our lives. As a result we find ourselves alienated and condemned.

The needed divine intervention ultimately comes through Jesus Christ. This is the good news of the Gospel.

The gravity of our condition is brought home to us not just by realizing the extent of our predicament but by considering the length to which God went in order to rescue us.

Only in the death of the Lord Jesus on behalf of sinners could God's justice be served and God's love conveyed. By faith we receive the gift of Jesus's law-keeping through faith for salvation from sin, which was perfectly achieved on our behalf, and in Him we become righteous. Therefore, we uphold the Law by turning our backs on our own warped efforts to keep the Law and by putting all our confidence and trust in the One who satisfied all the Law's demands on our behalf (Romans 3:31). We do not cancel the Law through this faith – we confirm it! A righteousness from God apart from law has been made known to us (Romans 3:21).

Thus, when one is saved through repentance of sin and faith in Jesus Christ, they are released from the power of sin and the condemnation of the Law. In salvation we are given new hearts to know and understand God's order for creation. The spirit of rebellion against the authority and rule of God is replaced by a spirit of obedience. Gospel-driven internal motivation replaces external moral constraint (Jeremiah 31:31-33; Ezekiel 11:19-20, 36:26-27).

This is good news indeed! What we are not able to accomplish, God has accomplished for us. To put it in a very contemporary form, God treated Christ as we deserved to be treated, so that He might treat us as Christ deserved to be treated.

Therefore, God's Law is still authoritative and necessary for Christians today. Jesus did not so much replace the Old Testament Law as make explicit its proper application to the heart and not just as an expression of external behavior

(Romans 6:14, 8:1-4). Jesus's idea of obedience moves beyond religious observance, focusing not only on the things we *do* but on who we *are*, as Jesus so clearly outlined in the classic Sermon on the Mount (Matthew 5–7). Only the gospel changes the heart and can lead to lasting change in our lives.

You will remember that when asked by one of the religious leaders to identify the greatest commandment in all of the Law, Jesus replied by quoting Deuteronomy 6:5 and Leviticus 19:18. "You must love the Lord your God with all your heart, with all your being, and with all your mind. This is the first and greatest commandment. And the second is like it: You must love your neighbor as you love yourself. All the Law and the Prophets depend on these two commands" (Matthew 22:37-40).

John Wesley saw this love of God and neighbor as the essence of holiness. Jesus says that if we truly love God and our neighbor, we will naturally keep the commandments. This is looking at the Law of God positively. Rather than worrying about what we should *not* do, we should concentrate on all we *can* do to show our love for God and others.

In many ways, Jesus's response about loving God and loving our neighbor summarized the heart of the Ten Commandments. This is the hinge on which all the Law of God hangs. As was mentioned, the first four of the Ten Commandments have to do with our relationship to God, while commandments six through ten address our relationship to one another. So, it's all about loving God and loving our neighbor.

Jesus came to fulfill the Law (Matthew 5:17). Jesus's purpose is to fill the meaning of the Law and prophets full, with the gracious purposes of God. Correctly understood, the Law and the prophets should lead to righteousness "greater

125

than the righteousness of the legal experts and the Pharisees" (Matthew 5:20). Failure to understand and live out this fuller meaning of the Old Testament will bring failure to "enter the kingdom." Jesus is the true Israelite who perfectly loved God with all of His heart and perfectly loved His neighbors (Luke 22:42; John 15:13). We are commanded to follow "in His steps" (1 Peter 2:21).

The Old Testament Law pointed to Jesus Christ and is only properly revealed in Him (Romans 8:3; 10:4; Galatians 3:24). In spite of the power of sin in the flesh and its ability to deceive the mind and distort the good purposes of the Law, Paul, both in Romans and Galatians, glories in the fact that God no longer condemns the sinner who is in Christ Jesus. Liberation begins with the saving action of God that has been accomplished by God's Son, Jesus Christ and is mediated by the Spirit. This saving action rescinds the sentence of condemnation that sinful humans deserve and sets them free from the onslaught of sin and mortality (Romans 8:2; 7:23-24).

Liberation is extended to Christ's followers in the form of the Holy Spirit, who becomes the new basis for their lives, displacing sin and selfishness. Because of the weaknesses and sinful propensities of human flesh, the Law proved unable to liberate people from sin and death, for people driven by the flesh cannot submit to the law or please God (Romans 8:3, 7-8).

However, Jesus Christ took on this same susceptible flesh (Romans 8:3) and defeated sin, overcoming fleshly selfishness through His own selfless acts (cf. Romans 5:15-19). Now, those "in Christ" may be empowered to live according to the Spirit (Romans 8:1, 4).

The Spirit ends the reign of fleshly selfishness for those who are in Christ because the indwelling Spirit works a moral transformation that empowers us to fulfill "the righteous requirements of the law." In other words, we may now live in accordance with God's will – the *requirement* of the Law – by fulfilling it through love, even though we are not bound to its every dictate (Romans 13:10; 6:14; 7:4-6).

While Paul insists that grace is the basis of our justification, he also expects Christians to live righteous and holy, sanctified lives (Romans 8:12-13; 6:18-19). For Paul, the Spirit empowers followers of Christ to think according to the Spirit and thereby directs them to life and peace.

In fulfilling the Law through His life, death, and resurrection, Jesus enables us to attain righteousness greater than that of religious obedience. Such liberation is achieved when we participate in Jesus's own life, death, and resurrection, a process that imparts a new life of righteousness. Those in Christ are liberated not only from sin but also from the jurisdiction of the Law.

John Wesley believed that the Law and the gospel are actually two sides of the same coin. When behaviors are commanded, they are law; when promised by God, they are gospel. Thus, the Law has *three uses*: convicting people of sin, bringing them to Christ, and then guiding them in their Christian life.

Although the Law is good and holy, sin weakened its guiding ability (Romans 7:7-8:4). Accordingly, God has now provided a more thoroughgoing remedy for sin and death by sending Jesus Christ and the Spirit.

In the New Testament, the apostle Paul made it clear that God sets us right on the basis of faith – in particular, the atoning faithfulness of Jesus Christ – rather than by works of the Law. Yet, if God's people are no longer under the Law, how are they to know what is right before God? While God liberates people from the dominating power of sin through Jesus and empowers them to live new lives by the Spirit, what does "obedience that leads to righteousness" look like (Romans 6:16)?

Romans 12:1 calls us to "present ourselves as a living sacrifice and to renew our minds." Here we can say that God's renewal of our minds reverses the earlier divine act by which we were relinquished to "defective" thinking (Romans 1:28). It instead enables us to discern the good, acceptable, and perfect will of God, which is of vital importance since, in Christ, God's people do not live "under the law" yet are to do what is loving and faithful before God.

In early Methodist history, John Wesley and his societies recognized the need for ongoing discernment and therefore asked their members, "What have you thought, said, or done, of which you doubt whether it be sin or not?" Setting an example for all Christians, they gathered weekly to encourage one another as they pursued transformation and the renewal of their minds.

I believe Romans 12-15 outlines a theology of "love, grace and faith" that provides practical wisdom to develop habits and virtues of "doing no harm" and "doing good" and "staying in love with God" as we seek to not only love God but love our neighbor.

The "law of the spirit of life" governs the believers' existence. All of this is possible because God in Christ dealt with sin – something that Law, allied to weak human "flesh", was incapable of doing. The condemnation of sin was experienced by Jesus so that the "just requirement of the law" (Romans 8:4) might be fulfilled in us. Believers are enabled

128

by the Holy Spirit to fulfill this just requirement of the law, summed up as engaging in loving actions for others. Believers are aware not only of freedom from slavery to sin but also of adoption to God.

So it is that in addition to our faith in Jesus Christ, love ought to define the Christian community and its members' actions. Rather than by the Law, God's people ought to live by the governing principle of love "from faith" (Romans 12:9-10; 13:8-10), which in fact fulfills the Law (Romans 13:10).

According to John Wesley's *Notes* on the New Testament, loving one another is a never-ending Christian obligation. It is also the essence of Christian ethics and behavior. When we avoid violating a particular law, the letter of the law is observed. But when we love one another, the underlying spirit of the law is fulfilled.

In John 14:15 and 21, Jesus links loving Him to obeying what He commands, so that love is the only Law in our relationships – with oneself, with neighbors, with enemies, with creation, and with God. In practice, it means promoting the highest good of others and not causing harm (*The Wesley Study Bible*).

Not only is the charge to love others the fulfilling of the Law, it is also filled with urgency since Christians "know what time it is" (Romans 13:11). The culmination of our salvation, the breaking of the eschatological day, is near (Romans 13:11-12). There is no time to indulge the darkness of our culture by partying, carousing, or fighting (Romans 13:13). Instead, we are called upon to "dress ourselves with the Lord Jesus Christ" (Romans 13:14). When we do this, we fully embody the transformation that begins with the renewing of our minds through Jesus Christ.

Dr. E. Stanley Jones said: "Many teachers of the world have tried to explain everything. They changed little or nothing. Jesus explained little and changed everything. Many teachers have tried to diagnose the disease of humanity. Jesus cures it. Many teachers have told us why the patient is suffering and that he should bear with fortitude. Jesus tells him to take up his bed and walk. Many philosophers speculate on how evil entered the world. Jesus presents himself as the way by which it shall leave. He did not go into long discussions about the way to God and the possibility of finding Him. He quietly said to me, "I am the Way.""

It's been said, "If a man goes to a psychiatrist, he will become an *adjusted* sinner. If a man goes to a physician, he will become a *healthy* sinner. If a man accumulates wealth, he will become an *affluent* sinner. If a man simply joins the church, he will become a *religious* sinner. If a man turns over a new leaf, he will become a *reformed* sinner. But he is still a sinner. But if we go in sincere repentance and faith to the foot of the cross, we will become a new creature in Christ Jesus, forgiven, reconciled, and set free to live."

Jesus himself said, "Desire [seek] first and foremost God's kingdom and God's righteousness, and all these things will be given to you as well" (Matthew 6:33).

To keep any of the commandments and forget God's love for us through Jesus Christ and our love for God is not to keep the commandments at all. It is simply to keep the Law. And that is a paltry thing indeed.

St. Augustine wrote, "We do not walk to God with the feet of our body, nor would wings, if we had them, carry us there. But we go to God by the affections of our soul." It is love of God, consciousness of God, awareness of God that is union with God. When all of life is permeated with such recognition, life is complete.

The new morality of Jesus breaks into the new dimensions of human relationships based on the ultimate demands of love.

Without the love of Christ alive in our souls, we are possessed by envy, ambition, rivalry, hate, and greed; and without the benevolent control of the Holy Spirit we toil on to our doom.

Law does not destroy love – it instructs it and guides it. Love does not destroy Law – it interprets, corrects and fulfills it. Law without love is not sufficient; struggle without love is not adequate: "A new commandment I give unto you."

Love is not an easy morality; love is a tough morality. Love forgives others but maintains a strong inner discipline.

As a friend of mine has printed on the back of his calling card: "If we meet and you forget me, you have lost nothing; but if you meet Jesus Christ and forget him, you have lost everything."

Positively stated and experienced, if you have Jesus in your heart, that is enough.

Simply stated, we are not to focus on the Law, but rather we are to focus on the Savior, Jesus Christ. It is only through a relationship with Jesus Christ that we can understand and live by God's Ten Commandments.

Noah Webster, a Founding Father of our country, told his students: "The first and great command is to love the Lord your God with all the heart and soul and mind and strength. This supreme love to God is the first, the great, the indispensable duty of every rational human being . . . . As the character of God is the only perfect model of holiness, it follows that all God's creatures who are intended to be happy,

131

must have the like character. But men will not aim to possess the character of holiness until they love it as the chief good. Hence, the necessity of loving God with supreme affections."

The Spirit of God longs for us to be Christ-like, and so be fulfilled. He wants the character of God to be evident in our lives. He wants for Christ to live in us and through us and flow out of us to others and guide our ways and our days.

A New Commandment: "That you love one another, as I have loved you." Impossible! Yet, we yield to Him, in whom all things are possible!

So, let's wrap it up right here. In fulfilling the Law through His life, death, and resurrection, Jesus enables us to attain righteousness greater than that of religious obedience. Jesus has delivered us from a slave master greater than Egypt — that of sin and death. Jesus was crushed under the weight of our sin so that we could be free to obey God's commands. Our gospel-empowered desire to obey God's commands creates a separate and unique identity for us as God's holy people sent out in His name into the world. Those who love God will express their love for Him in obedience and missionally in their love for others.

Charles H. Spurgeon, the great evangelist and often known as the "Prince of Preachers" in the 19th century and pastor of the Metropolitan Tabernacle in London for 38 years, encouraged his congregation along these lines when he wrote: "If we would at once overcome Satan and have peace with God, it must be by 'looking unto Jesus.' Keep your eye simply on him; let his death, his sufferings, his merits, his glories, his intercession, be fresh upon your mind; when you wake up in the morning look to him; when you lie down at night look to him. Do not let your hopes or fears come between you and

132

Jesus; follow hard after him, and he will never fail you."
(Morning and Evening: Daily Readings by C.H. Spurgeon).

That, dear reader, is how we live out these timeless truths for right living.

REFLECTION QUESTIONS

1. God has given us some helpful big-picture clarification concerning obedience to the law (Read Matthew 22:34-40 and Romans 13:8-10). Explain Jesus's statement in Matthew 22:40 and Paul's statement in Romans 13:10.

2. The only one who obeyed God's law perfectly was Jesus Christ; the rest of us fail. Many times too often. Only one violation is enough to condemn us (James 2:10). What is the good news we cling to in the face of such high expectations of holiness? (Matthew 5:17-18; Hebrews 4:14-16; Romans 8:1; 2 Corinthians 5:21; 1 John 1:9)

3. Read Exodus 20:12-17, Romans 13:8-10, and Romans 3:19-20. According to these texts, what three reasons was the law given?

4. What works of righteousness do you need to turn away from? In other words, how are you tempted to fill in the following blank: "I must/can pursue _____ in order to 'be good' or right with God." (i.e., family involvement, politics, spiritual disciplines, church or community service, a pure sexual ethic, competence at work, ethical integrity at school, the giving of money generously, etc.)?

HELPFUL RESOURCES FOR THE TEN COMMANDMENTS

Barclay, William. *The Ten Commandments.* Louisville: Westminster John Knox Press, 1973.

Begg, Alistair. *Pathway to Freedom: How God's Law Guides Our Lives.* Chicago: Moody Publishers, 2003.

DeYoung, Kevin. *The Ten Commandments: What They Mean, Why They Matter, and Why We Should Obey Them.* Wheaton: Crossway, 2018.

Chillister, Joan. *The Ten Commandments: Laws of the Heart.* Maryknoll: Orbis Books, 2006.

Collins, Kenneth J. and Robert W. Wall, eds. *Wesley One Volume Commentary.* Nashville: Abingdon Press, 2020.

Haines, Lee and Armor D. Peisker and Howard Hanke, eds. *The Wesleyan Bible Commentary, Volume 1, Part 1, Genesis-Deuteronomy.* Grand Rapids: William B. Eerdmans Publishing Company, 1967.

Kopp, Robert R. *God's Top Ten List: A Prescription for Positive Living.* Lima: CSS Publishing Company, 2001.

Martin, Glen S. *God's Top Ten List: The Ten Commandments.* Chicago: Moody Press, 1999.

Meilaender, Gilbert. *Thy Will Be Done: The Ten Commandments and the Christian Life.* Grand Rapids: Baker Academic, 2020.

Moody, Dwight L. *The Ten Commandments: Reasonable Rules for Life, Updated Edition.* Abbotsford: Aneko Press, Life Sentence Publishing, 2018.

Oden, Thomas C. and Joseph T. Lienhard, eds. *Ancient Christian Commentary on the Scripture, Old Testament III, Exodus-Deuteronomy.* Downers Grove: Intervarsity Press, 2001.

Packer, J. I. *Keeping the 10 Commandments.* Wheaton: Crossway, 2007.

Pope, Charles. *The Ten Commandments.* Charlotte: Tan Books, 2014.

Schoenhals, G. Roger, ed. *John Wesley's Commentary on the Bible.* Grand Rapids: Zondervan Publishing House, 1990.

The Wesley Study Bible. *New Revised Standard Version.* Nashville: Abingdon Press, 2009.

Tuttle, Robert G. *The Runway: Reflections on the Ten Commandments.* Lima: CSS Publishing Company Incorporated, 1997.